An open case

Library of social work

General Editor:
Noel Timms
Professor of Social Work Studies
University of Newcastle upon Tyne

An open case

The organisational context of social work

Joyce Warham
Department of Social Policy and Social Work
University of Keele

Routledge & Kegan Paul
London, Henley and Boston

First published in 1977
by Routledge & Kegan Paul Ltd
39 Store Street,
London WC1E 7DD,
Broadway House,
Newtown Road,
Henley-on-Thames,
Oxon RG9 1EN and
9 Park Street,
Boston, Mass. 02108, USA
Set in IBM Press Roman by
Express Litho Service (Oxford)
and printed in Great Britain by
Redwood Burn Ltd
Trowbridge and Esher

British Library Cataloguing in Publication Data
Warham, Joyce
An open case. – (Library of social work).
1. Public welfare – Great Britain
I. Title II. Series
361'. 941   HV245
ISBN 0–7100–8608–3
ISBN 0–7100–8609–1 Pbk

Contents

Contents

Preface

This book is written for social workers in training and at work, in the hope that it may help them as they seek to implement the ethical and humanitarian purposes of social work through roles which they have to carry, almost without exception, not simply as individuals in direct contact with clients, but as participants in formal organisations.

This purpose requires to be firmly stated at the very beginning, for it is not the intention either to present a social work point of view, or to make the assumption that social workers are the major determinators of the kinds of service which their clients receive. Some readers may find the approach adopted an uncomfortably iconoclastic one. On the other hand, it may be that the impact of the statutory and administrative changes of the early 1970s on social work in Britain, means that there is little danger of social workers viewing the world through their own professional rose-coloured spectacles, and attributing more power than corresponds to the reality either to themselves individually, or to the occupation of social work as a whole.

From whatever standpoint individual readers may start, the assumption which has determined the orientation of the book is that onlookers may see an important part of the game, and that 'professional' people may acquire a more realistic understanding of their working situations if they are willing temporarily to suspend their 'professional' perspectives, and to see themselves and the organisations in which they are employed as others see them: the others in this case being sociologists, political scientists, social administrationists, and the like.

Both the form which a book takes and the subject matter itself, however, must inevitably be both influenced and limited by the knowledge and experience of its writer, and by his or her personal values which in this case include a general although, as will become apparent, a not unqualified commitment to social work as a means of helping people in a complex variety of difficulties. It is impossible ever to adopt, let alone implement, a truly neutral approach, even if that were to be considered desirable; for whoever even attempts to do so is attaching a positive value to neutrality itself. In this case, commitment to the worthwhileness of social work means that the book will be permeated by ideas, both implicit and explicit, about what organisations offering social work services ought to be like. All this having been said, the intention is to adopt as detached an approach as possible. The aim is to encourage social workers to become onlookers of the game in which in all seriousness they have to participate, which is constituted of the organisational processes through which social work services are implemented, and which may be called administration.

The nature and significance of these processes will be explored in some detail in chapter 5. Before that stage can be reached, however, it is necessary to provide a context for it, by considering first the concept of professionalisation and its relevance to social work; second, the attributes of social services, of which social work is but one component; third, the attributes of formal organisations as social scientists have identified them; and fourth, management theory as a basis for the identification and implementation of administrative methods appropriate to particular purposes. The aim is to encourage an open-minded approach, and one in which the 'organisation', rather than either the 'agency' or a pre-conceived concept of professional social work, is for the time being at the centre of the reader's mental universe. The pursuit of this objective requires the development of dispassionate ways of looking at certain social institutions, and at social work as a constituent element of them. It should be possible for social workers to bring to this particular activity the detached yet concerned approach at which they aim in working with clients. Those who have been employed in other than social work roles, or in other types of organisation, may look to their own past experience for an outside view of social work, and for a 'non-social work' perspective on organisations and management. Everyone can attempt to see social work as it appears to relatives, friends, newspaper and television reporters, leader writers, contributors to correspondence columns, and so on. Those with a social science background may adopt the perspective of a sociologist or a political scientist, or whatever. The potential origins of a dispassionate approach are many and varied, and to be sought by each reader for himself.

Three particular concepts however underlie the perspectives on social work, on organisations and on administration which it is hoped that the book will serve to communicate. Identification of them here may help to provide a rationale for what is to follow, and some explanation of it, by revealing something of the ways in which the writer's mind has been working. They are the concepts of process, of systems, and of paradigms:

First, it is held that any social institution, such as a social service, or a system of local government, or a profession, is best to be understood as always in process of change: we are dealing with dynamic phenomena in dynamic situations. This means that we can never hope to know exactly what any actual social institution is like, for even while we are trying to track it down, it is already changing. It means also that there are no finite problems, and thus no final solutions. The point is put by Nathan Glazer with respect to social policy: 'It is illusory to see social policy only as making an inroad on a problem. There are dynamic aspects to policy such that it expands the problem, changes the problem, and generates further problems'.[1] In attempting to explain, or at least to clarify, the nature of changing institutions, the best that the social scientist or the management theorist can offer is frames of reference based on what appear to be their more stable attributes. Paradoxically, one of the constants is change itself, which is most realistically to be regarded as ceaseless. Underlying everything which follows is the idea that social work as an activity, the professional organisation of social work, social services, formal organisations and methods of administration, cannot be fixed at any one point in time. They are all essentially processes: to put it in other words, they are all 'things which are going on'.

Second, while social institutions are perceived as processes, they are also considered as systems, or sets of interconnecting parts. A 'system approach' offers a way of attempting to 'spell out in detail what the whole system is, the environment in which it lives, what its objective is, and how this is supported by the activities of the parts'.[2] But even if a professional association, or a social service, or an organisation is taken to be a system with its own component sub-systems, each is also a component of a system greater than itself: as for example, a Local Authority Social Services Department is part of the super-system of local government. David Silverman suggests that a system approach begins by assuming the interrelatedness of apparently isolated phenomena.[3] This is an assumption which underlies the discussion of any issue, topic or phenomenon throughout the book: none is to be taken as self-contained.

Third, the concept of paradigms has served during the writing of the book both as a means of ordering ideas and as an explanation of the ways in which ideas seem to organise themselves.

Paradigms are here taken to have two particular forms. They may constitute representations of actual phenomena. Thus, for example, Greenwood's *Attributes of a Profession*,[4] discussed in chapter 1, incorporates a paradigm of social work as a professional occupation. The compilation of the book has involved the selection of paradigms of this kind and the application of them to the construction of a paradigm of social work in an organisational context. But a paradigm in this sense of the term is only one particular mental representation of the thing which one is attempting to describe: alternative paradigms are always potentially available, and no one paradigm is ever totally comprehensive.

Nor, as knowledge is never static, can it ever be conclusive; and second, the term may be used of the ways in which knowledge advances and is organised. In this sense, a paradigm is an achievement in the development of knowledge, which is both sufficiently new as to attract disciples, and sufficiently open-ended as to leave new questions to be asked and new problems to be solved. It is of the essence of paradigms in either sense that they replace existing sets of ideas, and are themselves subject to replacement over time. Thus the Weberian paradigm of formal organisations as bureaucracies has given place to others; and the same can be expected to happen to any paradigm of social work which at present influences those who are concerned to develop social work theory.

Paradigms in both senses seem to be useful and perhaps unavoidable tools, both for the organisation of ideas and as bases from which advances in knowledge can be made. They may also, however, tend to impose limitations on our perceptions of phenomena which are, as has already been stressed, essentially dynamic; in relation to which qualitative as well as quantitative criteria are relevant; and about which it is never safe to assume that knowledge is ever either final or complete. The reader will do well to be alert to this tendency, and while attempting to be aware of the paradigms which he himself is using, bring his critical judgment to bear accordingly.

There is one additional point to be made by way of orientation. We tend to say that social work (as distinct from social workers) aims at helping people, and that organisations (as distinct from their members) have 'goals' or 'needs'. But the ascription of such attributes to the occupation of social work, or to a social service, or to an organisation, implies that these have concrete identities, and powers of thought and action. They are all, however, only mental constructs, which can neither think nor act. Such constructs are intellectual tools which we cannot do without if we are to systematise our thinking about the world in which we have to act. The constructs however, are not to be mistaken for the realities which they are but an attempt to represent.

Introduction

If social workers wish to explore the ways the organisations in which they are employed might be administered and developed as more effective instruments of purposes which social workers think they should serve, then material from a variety of disciplines, and in particular from organisation and management theory, has to be incorporated into the ways in which they perceive their own roles and positions. The orientation of literature focused essentially on the purposes and methods of social work as professionally defined, is of comparatively little help to social workers who wish to examine either the nature of their employing organisations, or their own positions as members of them. However, the types of organisation in which social workers are now finding themselves are such as to force the need for this kind of enquiry upon them.

In illustration, one might consider the concept of agency function, which perhaps derives as directly as any other in social work theory from the thesis that what social workers must, may, or can do is determined by the context within which they are employed. Particularly as it has been developed in the more esoteric literature of social case-work, this professionally generated concept provides neither an adequately objective approach to the analysis of the working situations within which social workers find themselves, nor a sufficient guide as to how those situations might be more effectively managed and developed to serve the human purposes to which social workers profess themselves to be committed. In practice, social workers are confronted with the fact that 'agency function' is by no means at professional discretion to determine and, moreover, that it cannot in reality be adequately defined by a description of the services which the agency is supposedly there to provide. The concept is all too easily used subjectively, in so far as the 'function' of a particular agency is differently described by different people. It is also used normatively, in that 'function' may be defined not in terms of what an agency is formally required to do, or is

1

permitted to do, or actually does do — and even these clearly differ from each other — but of the services which the definer thinks it ought to provide, and the purposes which he thinks it should serve.

To say all this is not to deny the considerable usefulness of this particular concept as one starting point for examining the nature of the organisations within which social work services operate. Nor is it here intended to underestimate its usefulness to practising social workers: for it may help them to understand both the limits of the services which they are employed to implement, and the potential extent of the range of services which they may legitimately offer to clients, and for which they may reasonably look to the agency for resources. However, it is precisely because it serves purposes such as these that the concept of agency function, as professionally developed, should be regarded more as a pragmatic guide to action in specific cases, than as an aid to objective understanding of what any one particular agency is really like, either in what it does collectively, or in what it makes it possible for social workers to do individually.

If the connotation of 'function' in the literature of social work begs relevant questions, the same might be said of 'agency'. To assume that the organisations within which social workers are employed can be adequately described as 'social work agencies', as professionally committed social workers are understandably predisposed to do, is to beg very large questions indeed. What in practice justifies the use of such a term to describe units of employment as disparate as a Family Service Unit and a Local Authority Social Services Department? It may be that in this case social work literature makes use of a concept which is congenial to social workers, and which implies what they themselves think that the organisations in which they are employed ought first and foremost to be, but which if accepted at its face value, may give only a one-sided picture of what some of these organisations are really like, and of the statuses and the positions of social workers within them.

An associated concept is that of 'setting', which also emphasises the significance of the working context as a determinant of the content of the social worker's role, and of the ways in which it both can be and, from a professional point of view, ought to be implemented. The notion has provided a conceptual framework for both the development and the teaching of methods of social work adapted, and adaptable to, a variety of working situations and (in the social work sense of the term) agencies. It facilitates the conceptualisation of fundamentally significant differences and similarities in social work as practised in different social services. It provides students with an anchorage in their mental and practical peregrinations in search of personally congenial contexts in which to be social workers. Thus, for example, the intending social worker is helped to learn in what ways, and why, the Probation Service on the one hand, and Local Authority Social Services

Departments on the other, constitute significantly different environments for the implementation of social work relationships; and that community work cannot be either described or implemented without reference to the ways in which it is shaped in practice by such fundamentally different settings as, for example, a Social Services Department or the Young Volunteer Force. Simultaneously, he will be led to examine what is common to particular methods of social work, and indeed to social work across methodological boundaries, in whatever services social work is practised.

However, neither the concept of agency function nor that of setting, even if they are considered together, seems to provide a sufficiently broad base from which to attempt to explain how or why individual agencies, within Local Authorities for example, or in the Probation Service, or in voluntary social services, differ from each other.

Perhaps the concept of 'supervision' provides a more appropriate starting point for this purpose: the process of supervision itself implies the existence of an individual, and therefore unique, relationship between student or social worker and supervisor; and administrative as well as professional elements enter into, and have to be recognised in, supervisory relations. Even here, however, as is certainly the case with 'evaluation', the emphasis in practice tends to be on the work of individuals, rather than that of the agency or organisation as such.

To isolate for comment only two or three concepts such as these from the whole literature of social work itself, and at the same time apparently to ignore the fact that social work theory is not taught in isolation from other disciplines such as sociology, social administration, or government, is possibly rash. But perhaps one general point is sufficiently valid to meet the case: social workers — theorists, teachers, students, and practitioners alike — interpret situations, develop ideas, and approach academic disciplines from within a professional frame of reference, and for professional purposes. Thus the perspectives of social workers on the organisations in which social work services are implemented are different from those of anyone else. In particular, concepts which have been developed by social workers themselves, or incorporated by them into social work theory from other disciplines, are intended to serve different purposes from concepts in for example, sociology, social psychology or political science. Whereas the social scientist is concerned primarily to understand, to explain, and to predict, the social worker whether theorist, teacher, or practitioner, is concerned first and foremost with the refinement of methods of work in a form of activity which is intended to serve consciously formulated ethical purposes. The concept of agency function may be used once more to illustrate this general point. Social workers will perceive, analyse, describe, and evaluate the units within which social work services are made available to clients, as agencies intended to serve purposes defined in social work terms. The social scientist on the other hand will consider them more neutrally as organisations, and will attempt to exclude from his study of them ethical criteria of his own about what they 'ought' to be doing. If such units are believed by social workers to be instruments (or agencies) intended to serve social work purposes, then a normative element both inevitably and rightly enters into any definition of their 'function'. The social scientist however uses the concept of 'function' to examine what an organisation actually does do, rather than to define what it ought to do. It follows that when a social scientist looks at an organisation in which social workers are employed, he may see something very different from what is seen by the social workers themselves.

What has been said so far has been intended to lend support to the view that both the theory and the practice of social work itself, as indeed of any other professional activity, are productive of perspectives on organisations which inevitably tend to be one-sided: as may be said to be the perspectives of doctors on hospitals, and of teachers on schools.

If social workers perceive themselves as members of 'social work agencies' and not of 'social services' or of 'organisations', they will see and understand much less of the full picture than is potentially available to them. Furthermore, by virtue of their training in the significance and management of personal relationships in the processes of social work itself, there may be a strong built-in tendency for social workers to perceive agencies – or indeed organisations – in terms of personalities to the exclusion of structures: or to put this in another way, to attribute behaviour to personality, but not to the organisational positions from which individuals have to act.

In one way or another, however, all theoretical approaches to the study of organisations are selective, irrespective of whether they are professionally or scientifically oriented, and they must be recognised as in some way biased: no social scientist can free himself from the limitations of his own 'view of the world', and there can be no 'grand theory' which takes everything into account. Furthermore, social workers are quite justified in selecting from the theoretical material available to them, from whatever academic disciplines seem to them relevant, that which seems to be most useful for their own professional purposes in particular situations. Nevertheless, between the intentionally positivist and analytical approach of the social scientist, and the practical, professionally oriented and committed approach of the social worker, there is the possibility of a third approach to the study of organisations and their administration, which it is a central intention of this book to encourage. This approach demands of social workers an ability to emancipate themselves from the bondage of a professional perspective, in order to examine what Rosemary Stewart has called the 'reality' of organisations, and of administration, with as much detachment as possible, while at the same time retaining and developing the capacity to interpret the significance of what they see, and its usefulness for their own purposes. This is not to say that all wisdom and understanding are vested in the social scientist, be he sociologist, or social psychologist, or whatever. Social workers can tell social scientists important things about certain types of organisation which they would not otherwise know, and the exchange of information and of ideas must clearly be a two-way process. For present purposes, however, emphasis is placed on the need for social workers to incorporate a positivist element into the ways in which they themselves perceive and interpret their occupational situations.

The expansion of potential channels of such exchange has been a noticeable development of the past few years. As suggested at the beginning of this introduction, social workers find themselves in positions in which they are forced to ask questions about the whys and wherefores of organisational structures and processes: they are becoming 'organisation conscious'. There has been an expansion of empirical research into the structure and administration of social work services. Teaching on organisation theory and on administration is being incorporated into both basic and advanced social work courses. A literature has developed in which the perspectives of both social work and sociology, in a variety of mixtures, are brought to bear on the types of organisation in which social workers are employed.

And thus we return to the purposes of this book. First of all, it is intended for social workers, whether students or practitioners, rather than specifically for administrators. While it is hoped that the material included may be useful from an administrator's point of view also, the main thesis is that social workers themselves, as well as administrators, require an understanding of the nature of organisations, and of administration as a process for maintaining and developing them. Whether or not it is a social worker's intention ultimately to move into an administrative position, as a social worker he is employed under organisational auspices, and needs to understand the implications of this for the performance of his social work role: which in any event he finds cannot in practice be separated from an administrative one. It is as an aid to such understanding, rather than as a handbook in administrative methods, that the book is planned to serve. The aim is to present an examination of the nature of professions, of social services, of organisations, and of administration, which can be used by students and social workers for the more objective analysis and discussion of their own immediate situations. In the long term, one would hope to see a more extensive incorporation by social work theorists of material from organisation and management theory into social work theory itself.

The book is intended to serve the purposes of social work, but it has deliberately not been compiled either from, or in order to give, a social work point of view. The intention is to offer a systematic approach to an extensive range of material which has no common source, and to illustrate its relevance to social work. Some of the material drawn upon was written by social workers, but much more of it is the work of social scientists and others who make mention neither of social workers nor of their agencies. The hope is that social workers will analyse what they read as objectively as possible before attempting to incorporate it into their own social work thinking: for as has been indicated already, a central intention is to encourage them, without in any way perjuring their own souls, to look at 'social work agencies' through other than social work eyes.

In essence, the aim is to make material which may facilitate the understanding of organisations and of administration more accessible to social workers, and to encourage its use. The main emphasis is on organisation and management theory, but an appreciation of the nature of social services is also essential if the forms taken by the organisations in which social work tasks are performed are to be understood. Enhanced understanding will not of itself produce either organisations or methods of administration which are more effectively directed to social work purposes: but it could be a contributory factor.

Chapter one

The concept of professionalisation

There is no expert group which does not tend to deny that truth
may possibly be found outside the boundaries of its private Pyrenees
H. Laski

Social workers are perenially concerned about their own professional
identity, and this is not surprising. For very many years, social work
training has been an acculturation process in which from the beginning
of their courses, students have been encouraged to think of themselves
as preparing to enter professional practice. At the same time, their
experience outside the training institution reveals that social workers
are not entirely free to define professional roles for themselves and,
moreover, that the kind of action which they may think that effective
help to clients demands, cannot in any case be confined within a
professional role as traditionally understood.

The idea that social work is a professional activity has pervaded the
literature and indeed the whole culture of social work, but is
exceedingly problematic in practice. Much current concern may derive
from the idea that professions are of most use to their own members,
and from a fear that emphasis on the professional nature and status of
social work may diminish social workers' capacity to put the needs of
their clients first. Additionally, much of it is centred on problems to do
with the implementation of what are believed to be professional roles
within what are perceived as bureaucratic settings. If it is particularly
for this second reason that it seems relevant to start this book with an
examination of the concept of professionalisation, the discussion of the
nature of social services and of public administration in chapter 2 will
duly emphasise that professional activity may also be shaped by the
public and the political, no less than by the organisational, nature of
the circumstances in which it takes place.

The first matters for consideration must be what is meant by the
term 'profession', and whether it can be said to have any objective

meaning irrespective of the aspirations of those who consider themselves to belong to a professional occupation. In other words, a
preliminary question is whether an occupational group may be said to
constitute a profession simply because it so describes itself.

It is taken for granted neither that social work undeniably is a
professional occupation, nor that the professionalisation of social work
either is or is not a 'good thing'. First it is hoped that an examination of
the concept of professionalisation may encourage social workers to
consider for themselves not simply whether social work is or is not a
profession, but rather in what respects this concept, which has so far
been so central to both theory and practice, is of use in helping them to
understand the nature of their particular occupation. Second, such an
examination may provide a basis upon which individuals can develop
their own conclusions about ways in which professionalisation may,
and ways in which it may not, be instrumental to the purposes which
they wish to serve.

The plan is to examine what is meant by a profession; to suggest ways
in which the nature of occupational groups which so describe
themselves can begin to be understood; to touch in a preliminary way
upon some aspects of the employment of professional people in
organisations; and finally to refer to the professional identity and status
of social work. To attempt to do all this is to imply that it is possible
to make at least some meaningful distinctions between professional and
other kinds of occupation. It is also to imply that it matters, at least in
some ways, whether or not the members of an occupational group
perceive themselves as professional people, and whether or not they
attempt to protect, to enhance or to restrain particular aspects of
professional development.

The nature of a profession

We are concerned at this stage with the problem of defining a
'profession', but before even this task is begun it seems relevant to
clarify both the purposes and the nature of definitions as such: for
similar definitional problems and purposes arise in relation to professions, to organisations and to administration. With reference to the
problem of defining social work itself, Helen Witmer wrote that the aim
of her enquiry was 'not to discover some *thing* that exists, but to arrive
at some *knowledge about* certain activities'.[1] By focusing on this same
purpose, as definitions are pursued in the course of this book, we may
hope incidentally to diminish the risk of endowing mental constructs
(such as 'organisation') with powers of action, which in reality are
attributes neither of professions nor of organisations, but only of
individual members of them. For example, when we say that a

profession has decided to do something, it would be nearer the truth to say that certain members of the profession have made this decision, the nature of the profession itself remaining elusive. With this distinction in mind, it may nevertheless be worthwhile to consider, for Helen Witmer's reason, what professions are like and what they have in common.

Social workers, or at least those who are trained, typically describe themselves as members of a 'profession'. They may even go so far as to join a 'professional' association and read a 'professional' journal. But a great variety of occupational groups, not all of which social workers would regard as professional, also so describe themselves, and have their own associations and journals, and even licensing systems to control membership. The immediate task is to consider whether the term 'profession' has any meaning which makes its use appropriate in respect of some occupational groups but not of others.

Two major kinds of approach, very different from each other, may be applied to this task. The first starts with the construction of abstract models intended to identify the distinguishing attributes of fully-fledged professions. In the second approach all occupations, including the so-called professions, are perceived as dynamic social processes and systems, internally heterogeneous, and continually evolving within changing social contexts: the significant question is not whether or not they are professions, but in what ways they, or sub-systems within them, have been or are becoming professionalised.

The 'ideal type' concept
The construction of an ideal type model constitutes an attempt to identify the attributes which are typical of particular kinds of social institution, such as formal organisations, or as in our immediate case, professions. Sociologically, an ideal type model is purely an abstraction: 'ideal' refers to a neutral set of ideas representing an archetype, rather than to a normatively constructed standard of excellence. Thus an ideal type model of a profession is intended to represent what a fully developed profession is like, rather than what, in any normative sense, it ought to be like. Furthermore, although an ideal type model may be a device for attaching a shared meaning to the term 'profession', no such model can provide a complete description of any occupation: it can only be partial, and it is always at one remove from any objective reality.

The building of an ideal type model of a profession involves the selection of a prototype profession which (like medicine) is universally acknowledged as such, and the abstraction of its major characteristics. Against the resulting model, the professionalism of occupations such as for example, plumbing, or accountancy, or social work, or hairdressing, or whatever, may be measured.

On the basis of the idea that professional occupations share attributes which distinguish them from non-professional ones, one such model is offered by Greenwood.[2]

The attributes by which he considers that professions in general are to be identified are, briefly, as follows:

(a) A systematic and internally consistent body of theory or knowledge, the acquisition of which requires intellectual as well as practical education, and which provides the base upon which skills and techniques are developed.

(b) Authority, with which the practitioner is endowed by his clients, not because of his official position, but by virtue of the theoretical knowledge, and its dependent practical skills, of which the profession has a monopoly.

(c) Community sanction which endows the profession with a monopoly of powers and privileges, such as the right to practise, to use a professional title, and to control admission to, and the content of, training courses.

(d) A code of ethics, part formal and part informal, which prescribes the bases of relationships between professional peers, and between professionals and clients; which acts as a check on the abuse of professional monopoly; which gives expression to the profession's commitment to the welfare of clients; and which serves to encourage the public confidence upon which the continuation of community sanction depends.

(e.) A professional culture generated within the formal and informal groups through which the profession operates, such as work groups, employing organisations, educational centres and professional associations, and which embodies the concept of a career.

These attributes which Greenwood lists, however, are not uniformly or exclusively the monopoly of the acknowledged professions, but are shared to varying degrees with 'non-professional' occupations; and herein lies one of the inadequacies of 'ideal type' models. Additionally, not all occupational groups which describe themselves as professional, share all of these attributes to the same degree. We should for this reason, according to Greenwood, think of all occupations as distributable along a continuum, at one end of which are bunched the undisputed professions, while at the other end are the least skilled occupations. Along the whole continuum are occupations which share to varying degrees the attributes by which professions are to be identified. The meaningful questions to which such a model as Greenwood's gives rise, are not whether plumbing or accountancy or hairdressing or social work is or is not a profession, but in what ways and to what extent any such occupational group either exhibits the various characteristics identified in the model, or desires to, or is capable of, developing them.

Furthermore, even if an analysis of both accountancy and social work, for example, shows them to share some characteristics in which they both approximate to such a model, we are as likely to be struck by differences between them as by similarities. It may therefore be useful to bear in mind the possibility of categorising professions, on the basis of characteristics which some of them share with others, or which differentiate them from the rest.

For example, Halmos suggests that a meaningful distinction may be made between 'impersonal service' professions and 'personal service' professions.[3] Although the members of professions such as medicine and social work, which he places in the second category, might well not agree with him that their task is to bring about changes in the personality of the client, it may yet be useful to recognise a distinction between professions of which the concern is primarily with clients as persons, and those in which activities are centred on the the resolution of problems of an impersonal rather than a personal kind, as perhaps in accountancy. Helen Witmer approaches the task of categorising professions from a somewhat different angle, while similarly emphasising the significance of the relationship between the professional person and the client: 'The characteristics that set any profession apart from others and constitute its uniqueness, are to be sought in the common ground where the needs of the clientele and the activities of the profession meet.'[4] Nina Toren provides an American illustration when she suggests that 'the nurse has a posture towards the patient that is less universalising than that of the physician. She emphasises the uniqueness of each patient, and his need for emotional contact'.[5]

Greenwood's model, of which only the bare outlines have been given here, may be compared and contrasted with others,[6] and evaluated as an attempt to represent the 'reality' of acknowledged professions. Attention must be given, however, not only to the substance of this particular model or to the measurement of social work against it, but to the nature and uses of ideal type models in general.

Such models have more than one use. First, as already suggested, they may be used neutrally as yardsticks against which the stage of professionalisation of particular occupations can be measured. Second, in so far as they are a representation of professionalism *per se*, they may serve as guides to the objectives which occupational groups seeking professional status need to pursue. Third, they may be used by interested occupational groups as a means of keeping in mind major aspects of professional development which merit continuous concern. The first of these uses is essentially analytical; but the second and third have to do not so much with the scientific understanding of what a particular occupation is like, as with the identification of objectives which its members may wish to pursue. When put to these second and third uses, an ideal type model ceases to be simply an analytical tool, and comes to stand for an example to be followed. Indeed it may well be that in lay as distinct from sociological use, the expression 'ideal type' is commonly assumed to refer not to an abstraction derived from empirical observation, but rather to a model representing a desirable goal. Greenwood, for example, developed his own model not simply to clarify the essential nature of any profession, but as a means of 'illuminating the goal for which social workers are striving'.[7] His model can be used either as an analytical tool, or as a statement of desirable objectives.

Although these uses of ideal type models can serve different purposes, each of which is enhanced if distinctions between them are kept in mind, they also have certain limitations. First, whatever the characteristics chosen for inclusion in a particular model, we cannot expect that a 'real' social institution will ever be found to correspond to such a pure type. Second, and perhaps more importantly (since we have to accept that no abstraction corresponds exactly with what it represents an attempt to describe), no ideal type model of a profession includes attributes of a non-professional kind which occupations which conform closely to the professional model may share with occupations which do not. For example some, although not all, professional associations share with trade unions the task of collective bargaining on behalf of their members. Thus to use an ideal type model as one's only frame of reference, is to run the risk of forgetting the non-professional dimensions of what may, according to the model, be undeniably professional occupations. The conclusion that medicine conforms closely to an ideal type model of a profession (for indeed it is often taken as the very prototype of a profession), may tell us a good deal about medicine as an occupation, but by no means everything that it is possible to learn. It tells us nothing, for example, about the pressure group or the 'trade union' activities of medicine's professional associations; or about the variety of organisational contexts within which medicine is practised; or about the existence of business as well as altruistic attitudes amongst its practitioners; or about status differences between sub-groups within the profession; or about changes in the profession over time. In effect, the ideal type approach to an understanding of the nature of a profession requires to be supplemented from elsewhere.

Professions as social processes and as systems

One of the apparently useful features of an ideal type model is that at least it offers a fairly precise definition. But if only because such a model may be used for normative as well as analytical purposes, the very possibility of arriving at an objective definition must be questioned. On this point, Cogan[8] considers that different kinds of definition are developed to serve different purposes. First, he suggests that some definitions are most accurately to be described as *logistic*. Here the primary intention is neither to persuade, nor to serve operational purposes, but rather to describe, and to ascribe precise meaning, so that those who use a term share a common meaning of it. Second, *persuasive* definitions are designed, or adopted, to argue a particular case. For such a reason, a model such as Greenwood's may be found congenial by social workers, in so far as it summarises the ways in which they would like their own occupation to be perceived and to develop. Third, *operational* definitions may be constructed in order to clarify and facilitate decisions which either the organisation or the practice of a particular occupation requires. Thus, for example, the long process of creating the British Association of Social Workers (BASW) out of a number of pre-existing associations (the Institute of Medical Social Workers, the Association of Child Care Officers, and so on), required the development of revised and refined operational definitions of professional social work appropriate to the creation of a co-ordinated profession, and the establishment of a unified professional association.

If definitions can be developed to serve different purposes, and should be assessed with the intentions of their originators in mind, it is also the case that any one definition may be put to uses other than that for which it was originally formulated. For example, taking Green-wood's model as one possible definition of a profession, we may interpret it either logistically, or operationally, or persuasively, depending on the purposes which we happen to wish it to serve at any one time.

All this indicates that no definition of a profession should be taken at its face value. We need to examine the purposes for which it was constructed, and the purposes for which we ourselves are using it. No definition can be adequately interpreted out of context; and the contexts in which definitions are developed and used are neither uniform nor static.

In discussing Cogan's presentation of the difficulties of attempting to arrive at a definitive description of a profession, Philip Elliott identifies two further problems. First he suggests that the title 'profession' needs to be interpreted as representing not so much a concrete state of affairs as a claim to social standing and recognition, or a symbolic label for a desired rather than an actual status.[9] The title is indeed used by occupational groups which vary considerably in the degrees to which and the ways in which they conform to any one of the 'standard' ideal type models. Individual members of these groups may believe that social status accrues from membership of a profession and occupational groups themselves may attempt to claim a professional identity as a means of enhancing their status, and their authority, in relation to the established professions with which their work brings them into contact. However, status cannot in reality be assumed. It can only be ascribed, and those who seek professional status can do no more than say to the outside world 'we are worthy of professional status for such and such reasons. Please ascribe it to us'. In hospitals, the statuses of social workers on the one hand and of doctors on the other seem to illustrate Elliott's point, as does the status of social work in general in the community at large.

Second, Elliott stresses that a profession is never a static pheno-menon, as ideal type models tend to imply, but rather a dynamic process, operating at the three distinct although interconnected levels: of social change, of professional organisation, and of individual careers. Elliott finds that some of the most interesting questions about the nature of professions have to do with 'professionalisation as part of general social change, the way different occupations aspire to and achieve professional status, and the ways in which individuals become practising members of particular professions'.[10] This point of view implies that the 'profession' of social work, like any other, is best understood as a process with an historical past which will extend, and indeed is already extending, into the future. It also implies that professions are not self-contained, but are shaped by changes in the social contexts in which their development takes place.

An interesting example of this approach is Reuben Bitensky's examination of the influence of changing social and political climates in the USA on the theoretical basis of social work itself. Bitensky's thesis is that while American social workers believe the profession itself to be in command of development in social work theory, the reality is that such developments constitute responses to social and political changes in the society in which the profession has continuously to redefine its role.[11] Another illustration of the 'social process' approach might take the form of an identification and analysis of the major events and developments preceding, surrounding, and following the passing of the Local Authority Social Services Act (1970), in terms of their influence on such 'professional' matters as professional organisation, the basis of specialisation in social work practice, patterns of social work training, the accreditation of courses, and the structure of social work careers. It is because change, both internal and external, is so significant for any professional occupation, that the dynamic concept of 'professionalisa-tion' rather than the more static one of 'professionalism' has been chosen for the title of this chapter.

Closely associated with the idea of professions as in process of continuous change, is an approach in which they are perceived as complex systems, or sets of structures and relationships, which are themselves sub-units of other and larger systems. Both the 'process' and the 'system' approaches are essentially sociological, in that they seek to analyse and to understand and interpret, rather than to imply the desirability of developments of any particular kind.

An example of these two approaches is presented by Bucher and Strauss in their examination of the nature of the American medical profession.[12] Unlike Greenwood, Bucher and Strauss are not concerned to illumine the goals for which the particular profession under consideration either is or ought to be striving. Rather, on the basis of empirical evidence, they formulate a process model, which presents a profession not, as in Greenwood's model, as a 'relatively homogeneous community whose members share identity, values, definitions of role, and interests', but as 'loose amalgamations of segments, pursuing different objectives in different manners, and more or less delicately held together under a common name at a particular period in history'.[13] The segments which Bucher and Strauss identify in the medical profession are not perpetually fixed parts of the body professional: they tend to be more or less continuously undergoing change. They take form and develop, they are modified, and they disappear. Movement is forced upon them by changes in their conceptual and ethical apparatus, in their institutional conditions of work, and in their relationship to other segments and occupations.[14]

Here is a picture of a profession as a system which is composed of possibly conflicting sub-systems, which forms part of systems wider than itself, and which is subject to processes of continuous modification in its internal structures and relationships. Bucher and Strauss conclude that the assumption that professions are homogeneous and stable groups is neither accurate nor useful, 'for there are many identities, many values, and many interests'. The position of many individual Probation Officers and of the National Association of Probation Officers in relation to BASW; the existence of special groups within BASW; and the attitudes of medical social workers towards their incorporation into Local Authority Social Services Departments in 1974, are only three examples of segmentation identifiable at one point in time in professional social work in Britain.

Bucher and Strauss present a concept of medicine as a profession by concentrating on the idea of the evolution and inter-relationships of internal sub-systems, segments, or specialties. For example, they suggest that specialties evolve around particular work activities, methods, and techniques; around sets of relationships with clients; and around ideas about what particular sub-groups consider their own particular mission to be. It is not difficult to apply their approach to an examination of the organisation of social work, and thus to reveal the heterogeneity and the changeability of what social workers may refer to as 'the' profession.

Bucher and Strauss focus on changes in and between sub-systems within a profession. Both Elliott and Bitensky on the other hand, emphasise the idea that the forms which the development of a profession takes constitute responses to external and changing social conditions. This implies that professions cannot be adequately defined or understood as systems which are self-contained or closed. They are open systems, which interact with other systems, which engage in exchange relationships with other systems, and the future development of which is inextricably linked with that of the other systems upon which the implementation of professional roles depends. Thus for example, in order to clarify the nature of the medical profession in Britain, one needs not only to consider its internal structure, but also to explore its interactions with the system, or complex of sub-systems, which is the National Health Service. The same point applies to social work in local government.

The gist of what has been said so far can be summed up as follows. Where the professional identity of an occupation is in question, it is relevant to ask not whether it is or is not a profession, but in what ways and to what extent the attributes identified in ideal type models do in fact apply to it. Professions in practice are not totally unlike other occupations, but share some characteristics with them. Like any other occupation, a profession is a social process or movement, which is in constant process of change within changing social, political, and technological and organisational contexts. Finally, like any other kind of occupational group, a profession is constituted of interacting sub-systems, and interacts with systems other than itself: it is neither homogeneous nor self-contained, and it is not in autonomous control of its own destiny.

The concept of a 'professional person'

If ideal type models have both constituted and influenced attempts to define the nature of a profession, so they have also contributed to the development of stereotypes of the 'professional person'. Working from Greenwood's model, we might arrive at such a stereotype: a professional person is one whose occupational activities, based on the monopolistic exercise of skills developed in relation to an exclusive body of theoretical knowledge, regulated by a professional code of ethics, and sanctioned by the community, are a personal responsibility for which he holds himself accountable to the profession of which he is a member and from which he derives his authority.

However, the exploration of questions related to each of the ideal type attributes of a profession which have been identified so far, indicates that an ideal type model of a professional person is no closer to the realities of the workaday world than is that of a profession.

What constitutes the body of knowledge, acquired through long and formal education, which a professional person is assumed to have at his disposal? How extensively is it shared and used by all members of the occupation, either at the completion of their formal education or during subsequent years of practice, and how exclusive is it to them? Similar questions may be posed in relation to professional skills. How formal is the code of ethics in accordance with which a member of a profession is said to work? What sanctions are there against those who violate it? How clearly is it understood by individuals? How do they, when there is conflict, effect reconciliations with their own personal value systems? What happens when work within a legislative or organisational framework, or in practice for private profit, gives rise to the need for compromises? Are there in fact no external checks on the ways in which members of professions do their work? May it sometimes be that the community sanctions not so much what the individual person actually does, as the activities thought appropriate to the position which he holds? Are members of a profession always accountable personally and exclusively to the profession for the proper implementation of their professional roles? What of the member of a profession who is employed in an organisation and is accountable to lay administrators; who must work within the formal limits of legislation and of statutory rules and regulations; and whose clients are allocated to him rather than selected by him? If a professional person is said to be one who derives his authority from the profession of which he is a member, what of the practitioner who does not join the professional association; or whose authority in at least some of his activities derives from the law, or from the position that he holds?

In addition to these and similar questions in relation to the professional role, it is also to be remembered that no one occupies only one role. The member of a profession may be also an employee, an officer of the court or of local government, a member of a religious denomination or of a political party, and so on. He may both derive authority from these other roles, and consider himself subject to authority from other than professional sources. An hypothetically pure professional role is diluted in practice by the other roles which individuals carry.

The posing of all these questions has been intended to indicate that complete conformity to an ideal type is not a practical possibility for individuals any more than for occupational groups. There is a dynamic element in professional activity as well as in the nature of a profession, and professionals participate in systems other than professional ones. As in the case of a profession, any attempt to define what is meant by a professional person may be used for logistic, operational, or normative purposes. In the first case, attempts at definitions are useful not because they are conclusive, but because the processes by which definitions are arrived at can help to clarify the nature of what are essentially imprecise activities, situations, and roles.

Whenever the concept of a profession is discussed in specific relation to social work, two problematic questions arise: in what ways may social work be meaningfully described as a profession, and in what ways does it matter whether or not it incorporates, or attempts to develop, the attributes typically ascribed to a profession? These two questions have a variety of implications for the activities and future development of any occupational groups with aspirations towards the attainment of professional status.

For example, it is possible that although characterised by a strong ethical commitment to the service of clients, which matters to it very much, a particular occupational group cannot achieve either the monopoly over practice or the autonomous professional authority which are attributes of a fully developed profession. At the same time, it can be argued that it may in any case not be a good thing that it should do so. Professional monopolies may be socially dangerous, and it may be desirable that the potential power of professions should be limited by the operation of a system of checks and balances in which laymen participate. This may be particularly the case when areas of specifically professional knowledge and competence cannot be easily defined because they are so extensively permeated with personal and social values. George Bernard Shaw suggested, perhaps not altogether facetiously, that all professions are conspiracies against the laity. Along the same lines, the constitutional historian Dicey warned that 'respect for experts ought always to be tempered by the constant remembrance that the possessors of special knowledge have also their special weaknesses'.[15] The point can be illustrated from the arguments that certain decisions in war are too important to be left to the military, and that the power of the medical profession over the deployment of medical resources and over the price of medical care may sometimes be too great. A leading member of the American Public Health Association, himself a doctor, has suggested: 'the country does not . . . accept that professional altruism and ethical principles are sufficient safeguards to protect the public interest in matters of health'.[16]

It may indeed be that both practically and ethically, full professional status as an occupational goal, and professionalism as an individual value, tend to impose straitjackets on the ways in which members of occupational groups perceive not only their own situations, but also the public good, and indeed the good of their clients.

The concepts of 'semi-profession' and of 'professional organisation'
Ideal type models of a profession are constructed by abstracting the characteristics of occupational groups whose professional identity and status are not in doubt, and which therefore in a tautological way reflect the attributes included in the models. This is the case with

medicine, inadequate though an ideal type model may be as a basis for the analysis of even such a clearly professional occupation as this.

Greenwood's discussion of the attributes of a profession concludes with the assertion that, at least in the USA, social work is already a profession, having too many points of congruence with the model to be classifiable otherwise, but that it is 'seeking to rise within the professional hierarchy so that it too may enjoy maximum prestige, authority, monopoly, which presently belong to a few top professions'.[17] Another concept and an alternative analysis are offered by Etzioni. His thesis is that there are certain occupational groups whose members describe themselves as professionals, which manifest the attributes of a profession in various ways and to varying degrees, and which aspire to full professional status, but which for socially induced reasons are inherently incapable of achieving a full professional identity and status comparable with those of, for example, medicine or law. Amongst such occupations, which Etzioni describes as semi-professions, are teaching, nursing, librarianship, and social work.

To those whose concern is with prestige, the term 'semi-profession' may be unpleasing. If however, the concept is used analytically, it may be found to embody ideas which help to clarify both the nature of certain occupational groups and their positions within the professional spectrum. Acceptance of the middle-ground position implied in the notion of a semi-profession, might also help to relieve the frustration and tension felt by occupational groups whose self-image includes entitlement to a professional status which society appears to deny them. It might, suggests Etzioni, enable them 'to be themselves'. Etzioni describes the semi-professions as a group of new professions, which differ from law and medicine in that 'their training is shorter, their status is less legitimated, their right to privileged communication less established, there is less of a specialised body of knowledge, and they have less autonomy from supervision or societal control than "the" professions'.[18] A further point, particularly relevant to the central topic of this book, is that practically all their members are employed in organisations, which impose restraints of two particular kinds upon their professional employees.

The first of these restraints has to do with authority, and Etzioni suggests that both the highly individual nature of truly professional activity, and the exercise of professional authority, are diluted by the administrative authority which is vested in the supervisors to whom 'professionals' employed in organisations are accountable. In the case of social work in Britain, one might add another factor: the political and legal authority which operates in situations where social workers are employed to implement social legislation. (See chapter 2.)

The second restraint identified by Etzioni are the ways in which organisations handle the knowledge which is seen by Greenwood as the source of professional authority. The relationship between professional and administrative authority is affected by the amount and kind of knowledge of which professionals in an organisation have a monopoly. The fully professional organisation, such as a university or a teaching hospital, produces and applies and conserves and communicates knowledge, through the activities of professionals who dominate the organisation's very goals. In the semi-professional organisation on the other hand, the major professional task is limited either to the communication of knowledge, as in the school, or to the application of it, as in the social service agency. Professional work in such organisations, according to Etzioni, is less autonomous than, and is related to the administrative function very differently from, the work in which academic staff of a university or the medical staff of a teaching hospital are engaged. Furthermore, some professionals may be employed in organisations such as industrial firms, in which their task is to supply management or other specialists with knowledge which is to be put to non-professional uses, over which those who actually produce the knowledge have no control.

Out of this idea of relationships between professional and administrative authority as a function of the organisation, control and use of knowledge, it is possible, according to Etzioni, to arrive at a categorisation of organisations on the basis of the positions and roles of their professional employees. Fully-fledged professional organisations are those of which the goals are the creation and application of knowledge, and in which professionals dominate the authority structure. Semi-professional organisations are those in which semi-professionals are employed to communicate or apply knowledge, and in which they are subject to a degree of administrative control. Non-professional organisations are those which, when they employ professionals, do so for the purpose of the organisation's non-professional goals. On this organisational basis one might distinguish, for example, between degrees of professionalism in chemists working on research in a university; teaching in schools; or employed in research or production units in industry. Their professionalism is not simply the result of their being chemists, but is a function of the organisational context within which they work.

The concept of semi-profession may be of practical use in facilitating an individual's comprehension of his situation as an employee, and of the status of the occupation with which he identifies himself. As already suggested, however, issues surrounding the pursuit of professional identity arise not only out of the reality of a situation, but from what is considered ethically desirable. For example, Toren[19] suggests that in a full profession the two core elements of systematic knowledge and professional ethics are congruous. In the semi-professions, such congruence is lacking: engineering has a body of scientific knowledge, but is without a cohesive code of ethics, while social work on the other hand, according to Toren, is ethically committed to a service ideal, but lacks a fully developed and distinctive knowledge base which is exclusively its own. On the basis of these incongruities, Toren concludes that both engineering and social work fit a semi-professional model. But she then identifies a consequential question which cannot be objectively answered, but is a matter for value-judgments: ought social work to pursue scientific knowledge at the possible expense of its humanitarian principles?

Any attempt to reach a more objective understanding of the professional nature and status of an occupation will be riddled with ethical issues such as this; and it can be argued that it is the ethical questions which should provide the bases upon which action is decided. The aim here, however, is not to explore these, but rather to concentrate on the nature of the impact of employment in organisations upon the roles of those who would describe themselves as professionals. Implicitly or explicitly, this topic will run right through the book.

The major point to be made at this stage is that employment in any organisation modifies the nature of relationships between professionals and clients. In their 'ideal type' form, professional roles are implemented in private, and the professional person holds himself responsible for, and accountable to the profession for, the standard of his own professional performance, which is an essentially individual activity. The impact of organisational employment upon professional activity may be judged good or bad in particular circumstances or for particular reasons: but that it exists cannot be denied.

However, organisations are not homogeneous and as we have seen they may, according to Etzioni, be typed according to their professional or other purposes, and the status accorded to professionals within them. Etzioni finds the crux of the matter to lie in an organisation's authority/accountability structure, and distinguishes between a professional structure on the one hand, and an administrative (or organisational one) on the other. It is in accordance with this basis of distinction that he differentiates between professional and administrative acts:[20]

> ... the ultimate justification for a professional act is that it is, to the best of the professional's knowledge, the right act. He might consult his colleagues before he acts, but the decision is his. If he errs, he will still be defended by his peers. The ultimate justification of an administrative act, however, is that it is in line with the organisation's rules and regulations, and that it has been approved — directly or by implication — by a superior rank

Etzioni's concept of semi-profession is based on the idea that full professional authority is compromised by employment in other than fully-fledged professional organisations. His categorisation of organisations, however, need not be taken as hard and fast. Members of what he would describe as a semi-profession may work in a variety of organisations between which the differences are easier to identify than are the similarities. In the case of social work, for example, one might ask what organisational similarities it is possible to find between a Family Service Unit, a Child Guidance Clinic, and a Social Services Department. Moreover, there may be internal differences between organisations of the same general type and, most importantly, semi-professional organisations may vary in the extent to which professional authority permeates the administrative structure, with the result that the postulated distinction between administrative and professional acts is blurred. Additionally, there may be sub-units within every non-professional organisation where professionals retain a very high degree of autonomy. This is a point which perhaps also serves to illustrate the idea that organisations, as well as professions, are more realistically to be regarded as complex systems than as homogeneous units.

To make these qualifications is not to deny the usefulness of Etzioni's concepts. It is rather to suggest that in any formal organisational context, the pursuit of professional status calls for continuous and varied adjustments between professional and administrative authority. Doctors in private practice, or in general practice within the NHS, are professionally autonomous in ways that those who are employed under contract of service never can be. On the other hand, although a particular organisation may be meaningfully described in Etzioni's terms as semi-professional rather than professional, it is not to be taken as being immune from professional influence, which those of its members who are professionally committed will seek to exert upon it.

Professionalisation and social work

So far, the epithet 'professional' has been identified as applicable to occupational groups, to individuals, and to organisations. It may also be used to describe statuses in which individuals perform certain activities, as in the case of professional as distinct from amateur sportsmen, or social workers who are in employment as distinct from volunteers; or to describe the competence with which a job is done, as when we say that a 'do-it-yourself' handyman painting the house, or an untrained social worker supporting a family in a crisis, has done a professional job; or to describe behaviour, as in attempts to distinguish professional acts from administrative ones. The aim has been to illustrate some problems of definition, and to identify concepts without the use of which any discussion of the professional nature of a particular occupational group is likely to be unrealistic. The major points which it is hoped will have emerged are that professions cannot be said to exist in any homogeneous or finite state, and that to ask whether any one occupational group does or does not constitute a profession is to pose too simple a question. To understand what an occupation is like 'professionally' we need rather to ask what forms its professionalism currently takes, what are the possibilities that it will be able to maintain or develop particular professional attributes, what are its aspirations, and so on. To sum up, we need to interest ourselves in the ongoing process of professionalisation which takes place in changing social, political and technological environments, which themselves continuously influence the forms which professionalism takes at particular times or within particular cultures. To give but one example, the forms which clients' problems take, including the ways in which those problems are defined by clients themselves, by 'society', and by professionals, change over time; and so do the knowledge, the skills and the ideologies which professional people bring to their work, and the organisational contexts within which that work is done. Any analysis of any profession requires that any ideal type model is construed dynamically, and that it be recognised that no such model can be comprehensive. The component parts of any model must be interpreted in relation to changing social contexts, and in the light of the idea that an occupation both constitutes a social process and forms part of a network of changing social systems. We need also to distinguish between, and to recognise connections between, the analytical and the normative uses of ideal type models themselves.

Now, by way of illustration, we may consider how one might go about analysing the professional nature of social work as an occupation in, say, the Britain of the mid-1970s, using ideas which have been presented in the course of this chapter.

Effective analysis of any one of these ideas is not possible in isolation from the others, and there is no one logical order in which to try to use them. We might, however, begin by considering whether all professions are similar in kind as well as in their degree of professionalisation, or whether as Halmos suggests is the case, it is possible to classify them on the basis of any major distinguishing features. Bearing in mind Helen Witmer's insistence on the significance of the nature of the relationship between professional person and client in any profession, we might consider where social work stands in relation to Halmos's distinction between 'personal service' and 'impersonal service' professions. We shall need to be aware of possible overlapping between conclusions based on empirical evidence on the one hand, and those which derive from our ideas about what we consider it desirable that social work should be like on the other. However, from a consideration of the question whether or not there can be anything meaningfully called social work which is not based on the concept of personal service, we may both make some inroads into a sociological understanding of the ideological orientations of professional social work, and also dispel some of the confusion which is likely to arise when both social work and, say, engineering are combined under the general rubric of professional occupations.

Having explored the possibility that professions may be typed as differing in kind as well as in their degree of professionalisation, and that social work as a profession may manifest the characteristics of one type rather than another, we might find it useful further to consider the nature of social work as a profession by using an ideal type model such as Greenwood's. If the model is used as an analytical tool rather than as representing certain desirable objectives, it will force consideration of a range of questions about what social work is actually like, as distinct from what we think it ought to be like.

It will be advisable at this point, however, to formulate some preliminary ideas about what constitutes the subject for analysis. In medicine, one is either a doctor or one is not. The expressions 'social work' and 'social worker', on the other hand, are popularly used in relation to widely varying kinds of activities, performed by such a variety of people as the untrained volunteer, the salaried and experienced but untrained member of an agency, and the inexperienced but formally qualified graduate. The restrictions which apply both to the use of the title 'doctor' and to the practice of medicine do not apply, at least as yet, in the field of what is loosely called 'social work',[21] within the spectrum of which may be found very wide variations indeed in conformity to an ideal type model of a profession. We have to consider whether we will base our idea of the 'social work profession' on a particular occupational group and its sub-systems, and whether there are particular activities which can be said to constitute professional social work, and the performance of which legitimates the ascription of the title 'professional' to the social worker involved. It may be that in the practice of social work, a 'professional' act is extremely difficult to isolate,[22] and that an attempt to define professional social work by examining what even qualified social workers actually do, may give rise to more questions than answers. Perhaps all that can safely be said as a brief preliminary to the use of an ideal type model of a profession is that it has been customary for social workers who are formally trained and certificated to regard their kind of social work as professional, and themselves and their peers as professional persons. For present purposes we may take trained social workers as constituting the prototype of social work as a profession to the analysis of which the kind of question to which Greenwood's model gives rise may be relevantly applied; but particularly as this would not correspond to a 'popular' conception of social work, we shall have to bear in mind that we are begging very large questions indeed.

Is there a body of knowledge which social work as a profession can claim as exclusivly its own?[23] To what extent do social workers share this knowledge, and in what ways do they depend upon it in their work? Are there skills based upon this knowledge which social workers know how to use, and which are possessed by no one else? Is there an ethical code with which all social workers are familiar, by which they consider themselves to be bound, which is viable in the working situations in which they are employed, and for breaches of which the occupational group may punish its members? What is the status of social workers in the community? Are they perceived as professional people by virtue of their special knowledge and skills, or rather as officers of the court or of the Local Authority, or whatever? Do they derive their authority from professional knowledge and skills, or from the positions which they hold? How are limits set to this authority? Are social workers accorded rights of privileged communication? In what senses, and to what extent, may there be said to exist a professional culture, of either a formal or an informal kind?

An examination of questions such as these, which are prompted by the use of an ideal type model, will reveal something of what professional social work is like at any particular time. It will not, however, necessarily lead to the clarification of factors within it, and of influences upon it, which might be described as extra-professional, and which modify its nature. The use of an ideal type model thus needs to be supplemented by an examination of, for example, the possible impact upon social work as a profession of such phenomena as the co-existence of altruistic and career-centred purposes in both in-dividuals and in professional organisations; the co-existence of sub-groups of differing statuses within the occupation as a whole, or at the boundaries of it; and (the central theme of this book) the employment of social workers in a variety of organisational contexts, and within public social services.

Once an ideal type model is accepted as inadequately comprehen-sive, and social work as a profession is perceived as being influenced by factors of a non-professional kind, it is practicable to make use of Elliott's idea that professions are modified at the levels of social change, of professional organisation, and of individual careers. First, an attempt can be made to understand social work as an institution which has been evolving in a symbiotic relationship with a changing society, for the last hundred years or so. As a specific example, one might take the impact upon it of the changes in the social climate which took place during the 1940s and which produced the major social policy reforms which provided the context in which post-war social work had to develop. Second, it is possible to identify and analyse the impact of social change upon professional organisation. At the risk of some over-simplification, it can be suggested that the pattern of professional organisation in social work in Britain has broadly followed the development of particular statutory social services. One may, for example, ponder upon possible connections between the imminent restructuring of the personal social services, and the creation of BASW (with NAPO outside it) in 1970.

The 1970s have seen a coalescence of separate professional associations, but there is no reason to suppose that an existing pattern of professional organisation, either formal or informal, is any more final than those which preceded it. Current debate both about the professional status of the Certificate in Social Service and about whether community work is or is not social work, illustrates very clearly both the subjective and unstable nature of any definition of social work and the consequential organisational uncertainties.

The organisational structure of professional social work is continuously being modified by extra-professional forces, as well as for professional reasons. We may ask what forms of specialisation are at present in process of development; in what ways the professional statuses and positions of particular occupational groups (such as residential social workers or home-helps) will be modified as training programmes are developed for them; how the role of BASW as a professional association is developing in relation to the role of the Central Council for Training and Education in Social Work as an accrediting body; how BASW functions to protect its members as well as their clients; and so on. Third, the modification of social work as a profession is similarly visible as the micro-level of individual careers. Here we need to consider such factors as changes in the structure and content of training courses, at both basic and post-qualification levels; changes in the structure of the social services; and the mobility of labour within the whole range of employment, given particular political and economic conditions. Greenwood's concept of a professional culture embodies the idea of a career structure: and the implementation of the Local Authorities Social Services Act (1970), the reorganisation of probation areas as part of the restructuring of local government in 1974, and the simultaneous restructuring of the National Health Service, are but three examples of changes which have modified the employment situations within which individual social workers pursue their careers. One by-product has been the opening up of career possibilities in administration, as distinct from social work practice, with consequential concern about a career structure — or about the absence of it — for field workers.[24]

Elliott's idea that professions are modified at these three levels does not conflict with the use of an ideal type model as an analytical tool, but can supplement it. It still has to be borne in mind, however, that in considering the ways in which social work approximates to an ideal type model of a profession, one may be in danger of distorting reality. A predisposition to make use of such a model may be predominantly ideological, and there is a risk that the use of other frames of reference which might take one some steps nearer the reality may be overshadowed.

Etzioni's concept of semi-profession, embodying the idea that some occupations with professional aspirations have to be recognised as significantly different from the 'fully fledged' professions, provides an alternative approach. Instead of offering an abstraction as a starting point, it focuses attention immediately upon the real-life situations in which these occupations, amongst which he includes social work, are practised. The use of the concept of semi-profession as developed by Etzioni may serve to focus attention on the significance of the length of training for social work; upon the extent to which, and the ways in which, its status is legitimated; upon its right, or lack of it, to privileged communication; upon the nature and content of its specialised body of knowledge. Essentially, however, Etzioni offers a way in which one can look at professional social work as it is affected by the statuses of social workers as employees, and by the nature of the organisations within which they are employed. If Etzioni's thesis that the nature of professional activity is modified by the organisational context is accepted as valid, it provides yet another indication that social work as a profession can be neither homogeneous nor autonomous. If freedom from legislative or administrative or political controls is taken as an attribute of professionalism, then social work in some settings may be more 'professional' than it is in others.

Associated with the idea that the professional nature of social work can be understood only if we take into account the organisational contexts within which social workers work, is the notion that the roles which they perform may also modify the professional nature of the work which they do. What comparisons is it possible to make between, for example, the roles of Probation Officer and Family Service Unit worker, or between the roles of social workers in Child Guidance clinics on the one hand and an agency such as the Young Volunteer Force on the other? The significance of the varied organisational positions from which social workers attempt to provide services to clients is crucial to any attempt to understand the nature of social work as a profession.

The discussion of the nature of professions in the first section of this chapter was not intended to present finite definitions, and the subsequent very brief consideration of aspects of professionalism as they relate to social work has certainly not offered any conclusion about current problems. The aim has been to illustrate how a theoretical approach may be applied to the examination and clarification of existing situations.

Whereas, however, the sociologist makes no prior assumption that professionalisation either is or is not a 'good thing', and likewise offers no conclusions on the matter, social workers are not likely to be so impartial. Nor, it must be said, is there any good reason why they should be. Throughout this chapter, emphasis has been placed on the usefulness of a sociological or dispassionate analysis of the condition of social work as a profession. First, it may help to clarify the realities of the situations in which social workers have to implement their roles; but second, and perhaps more fundamentally, it may facilitate the making of better-informed and more rational value judgments. On this second count, a dispassionate approach need not imply a betrayal of one's commitments, but can constitute a means by which commitments may be more rationally decided upon, and perhaps modified.

If the situation is looked at analytically, it may have to be acknowledged that social work in Britain cannot ever be expected to reach equality with medicine in its degree of professionalisation. It may be that adherence to a concept of professionalism such as that which for so long was so dearly cherished by the Association of Psychiatric Social Workers and the Institute of Medical Social Workers, and which was certainly based on a medical model, is unrealistic and inappropriate in the 'reorganised' social service world of the 1970s. Nevertheless, within the limits of what seems possible, value judgments remain to be made about the desirability or otherwise of particular aspects of professionalisation. Authoritative figures are difficult to find, but it has been estimated that throughout the country the proportion of social workers in Local Authority Social Services Departments who are trained varies from 90 per cent to below 20 per cent; that, overall, fewer than 40 per cent of social workers and seniors are trained; and that three out of five are ineligible for membership of social work's professional association.[25] In such a situation, debate on 'open' eligibility for membership of BASW is only one manifestation of the controversial nature of the professional identity which for the APSW and the IMSW was both comparatively easily definable and a largely unquestioned value.

Conflicting values surrounding the idea of professionalisation are likely to remain central to much debate both on how social work ought to be defined, and on how social workers ought to organise themselves. At one extreme, some will judge professions to be closed shops, serving to protect their members and inhibiting adequately forceful intervention on behalf of clients. Others will argue that professionalisation is necessary to protect standards of knowledge, skills and ethics, and that it constitutes the best guarantee of clients' welfare.

Whatever decisions may in time be made on eligibility for membership of BASW, however, it is probable that no understanding of the current nature and condition of social work as an occupational activity is possible without reference both to the concept of professionalism and to the process of professionalisation, to which social work educationalists and trained practitioners have attached so much importance over so many decades. The selection of professionalisation as the introductory topic in this book, constitutes an assertion that the concept is relevant both to the social worker's comprehension of the nature of his occupational role, and to his views on how he should implement that role. Whether or not he himself either qualifies for or aspires to professional status in the traditional sense, the concept may be useful to him as he attempts to discover what there is of importance in the work which he does which cannot be contained within political or organisational frameworks but which he shares, or believes that he ought to share, with his peers.

The way in which the nature of a profession has been presented may also serve to emphasise that professionalisation as an objective need not be, and indeed cannot realistically be, accepted or rejected lock, stock and barrel. The task, both individually and collectively may be two-fold: to identify the factors which limit unrestrained professional development and to discriminate between those aspects of professionalisation which it is considered desirable to protect and if possible to develop, and those which should be held in check.

Chapter two

Social services and public administration

> The purposes of the social services are determined for them by the political and moral conceptions underlying the structure of the modern state, and their methods are equally decided by the philosophy of the age in which we live.
>
> T. S. Simey

Social work has dimensions other than professional ones, and as an ideal type model is an inadequate base from which to attempt to understand the nature of a profession, so the concept of professionalism is too narrow to embody the nature of social work. If professionalism constitutes one element in a social worker's role so, as the sub-title of this book emphasises, does his employment as a member of an organisation. But there is another factor which both directly influences the character of the work with clients which social workers regard as the core of their professional activities, and shapes the organisations within which they are employed. This is the nature of social services.

The development of social services and that of social work have interacted with each other from their very beginnings. An understanding of their interdependence, and of the nature of social services as a particular type of social institution, is a prerequisite of any effective analysis by social workers either of their roles and positions within individual organisations or of social work as an occupation. What social workers call 'agencies' are organisations which are components of either statutory or voluntary social services. It is of the nature of social work in contemporary Britain that it is not viable apart from such services. Nor is social work co-extensive with those social services of which it is a part: for that is logically impossible.

One obvious point is that it is not only those who hold positions as social workers who mediate services directly to their users. For example, in a Local Authority Social Services Department, other specialist staff such as occupational therapists, day nursery nurses, craft instructors and so on, may be implementing, for large numbers of people, specific services in the direct provision of which social workers may only intermittently intervene. If one takes into account not only the variety of specialist skills involved in the implementation of the full range of services administered by such departments, but also the nature of the services themselves (including for example residential accommodation for the elderly, meals on wheels and home help services) then social work, certainly as professionally trained social workers perceive it, takes its place alongside other methods of providing services to people who are in need of either skilled help or practical assistance or of somewhere to live. Additionally, there is of course the difficulty of defining the nature of social work itself within a social service. Is it to be understood as consisting of the work undertaken by all who hold the position of social worker, or by those who are professionally trained, or by those who consider themselves to be doing social work even though the title of social worker is not formally ascribed to them? And is everything that trained social workers do *ipso facto* social work?

Moreover, social services serve societal functions and purposes much broader than that provision of services to individuals which social workers might regard as adequate justification for a service's existence. It is on these other aspects of social service that this chapter will concentrate.

The nature of social as distinct from economic policy, and of voluntary as distinct from statutory social services, has been discussed on broad fronts elsewhere.[1] Here the intention is to concentrate on those features of social services which most strongly influence the *organisational* environments of the social workers who are employed under contract of service within them, and most of the chapter will be devoted to a consideration of certain major aspects of statutory services. This review may itself provide a basis for a comparative approach to the analysis of the nature of voluntary social services, but some specifically significant similarities between the two sectors, as well as some differences, will be discussed in a final section of the chapter.

Statutory social services are no more homogeneous than are professions. For example, in some of them no social workers at all are employed, while in others social workers are in the 'front lines' upon which the implementation of the service itself depends. However, even in the 'personal' type of social services, epitomised by Local Authority Social Services or (in Scotland) Social Work Departments, where social workers may perceive themselves as the embodiment of the service, four characteristics of all statutory (and not exclusively social) services influence, and are intended to influence, what social workers must, may, cannot or may not do. These are the interrelated phenomena of public sponsorship, public financing, public control and public administration. Each of these will be considered in turn.

Public sponsorship

This manifests itself predominantly through the formal political processes which culminate in legislation, and without which no statutory social service can either come into existence or survive. Whether particular statutes are more realistically to be seen at one extreme as representing an expression of the 'general will', or at the other as reflecting the efforts of small but powerful pressure groups, the fact remains that they are created by Parliament on behalf of the community, in response to publicly expressed and acknowledged need or demand, and that they are intended to serve social and political purposes which may be either more or less clearly defined. In the final event, the enactment of legislation is a political as distinct from a professional or administrative activity; and whatever part the pressure group activities of professional people may have had in influencing the form which legislation takes, the purposes which an Act of Parliament is intended to serve are much wider than those of any profession which may be interested in or affected by it.

This is so even if the co-operation of a particular profession is essential to its implementation. For example, the passing of the National Health Service Act (1946) was not to do with the organisation of health care alone. The Act was part of an extensive programme of social reform embodying values attached to the provision of services and the meeting of need on a social as distinct from a market basis, and on a much wider front than a medical one. In a sphere which social workers might regard as particularly their own concern, legislation relating to the care and protection of deprived children provides another example. The Children Act (1948), while laying the foundations for a service intended to be implemented by social workers, also provided that it should be the Local Authority (and not the Children's Department or any of its employees) into whose care a child should be received: the intention was to protect the value of public as distinct from professional responsibility. Additionally, this and similar legislation may be said to embody certain values concerning both the rights of parents and the liberty of the subject, which find expression in the allocation to the courts, rather than to social workers, of the authority to order a child's removal from home. Much of the debate surrounding the Children and Young Persons Act (1969) has centred on the question of the 'balance of power' between magistrates (primarily as defenders of justice and of individual liberty) and social workers (as non-judicial interpreters of what is best for the individual child). Such issues and their resolution belong in the last resort to the political domain in which formal relationships between state and citizen are established.

It is only within the basic framework of such relationships that legislative sanction is accorded to the professional activities of social workers employed in statutory services.

The practical significance of public sponsorship, expressed in the policy decisions of governments, is clearly visible in situations such as that in which social workers have striven to implement the original intentions of the Children and Young Persons Act (1969). This controversial Act of Parliament was passed by a government which very soon went out of office. Certain major provisions of the Act were opposed in principle by the succeeding government, which decided not to sponsor their implementation. Once public support in the form of government commitment was withdrawn, social workers were left with the task of attempting to implement a severely emasculated piece of legislation. Moreover, whatever the implications of the situation from a professional point of view; however serious the implications of such changes in policy for the provision of rehabilitative services for young offenders may be considered by social workers to be; and however strong one's own commitment to the intentions and methods of the Act as originally passed, the change in government policy has to be seen in the light of the constitutional principle of the supremacy of Parliament, and of the fact that no government is constitutionally bound to maintain the policies or the legislation of its predecessor. This point is stressed in order to emphasise once again that within statutory social services, issues which social workers identify as being of essentially professional significance, and as demanding professional action on their part, may have other far-reaching implications of an essentially political or 'public' kind.

However, the point that social legislation is created out of political processes, to serve purposes much wider than, and possibly conflicting with, those of the professions involved in the implementation of particular social services, is a fairly obvious one. More subtle are the interpretations which may be placed upon the epithet 'social' as applied either to legislation or to services. One interpretation would be that 'social' legislation and 'social' services are identifiable as such by virtue of purposes which have to do with the promotion of welfare. It is necessary however to consider whose welfare is in question, and to take into account the idea that publicly sponsored provision for the welfare of any individuals with whom social workers are primarily concerned, tends to be of a kind which is believed by the elected representatives who promote it, to be compatible with their ideas about the welfare of society 'as a whole', or about the interests of particular sections of it. It also reflects public opinion about the risks which it is desirable, or expedient, or possible to run; and about what financial resources should or can be made available. On this count also, the Children and Young Persons Act (1969) was and is controversial, provoking sustained debate about the potential effect upon the crime rate of treating young offenders as 'children in trouble'. Viewed from another angle, 'social' legislation is like any other legislation in that its origins are public; and the same may be said of statutory 'social' services, which are manifestations of publicly expressed concern, and the product of public, political, and social action.

In the case of statutory as distinct from voluntary social services, any 'social' action is indeed essentially political, in so far as it is aimed at influencing government policy, and is directed through political processes and institutions to the establishment, maintenance, and development of services which are legislatively sanctioned. Such sponsorship means that professsional employment in statutory social services has dimensions which can only be described as political. These will be referred to later, in the course of discussion of the forms taken by public and social control of social services, and of public administration. Suffice it for the moment to say that they are not essentially of a 'party' kind even in situations upon which the influence of party politics is strong. Nor does it follow that what has come to be called 'political activism' is intrinsic to the social worker's role as an employee, although he personally may choose to make it so.[2] However, when a social worker in a statutory social service acts to help a client, he does so on behalf of the community, with resources (including his own skills) made available and paid for by the community; and he is accountable through his seniors to the community's representatives (whether elected or appointed) for the work he does. It can be argued that as well as being held accountable, he should also consider himself 'publicly' as well as 'professionally' responsible, and that he thus faces the never-ending task of deciding how he should use the discretion available to him in the implementation of any aspects of social policy, expressed by statute or administratively, with which professionally or personally he may not agree. For this reason, this may be an appropriate point at which to refer briefly to the multiple roles which social workers in statutory social services may carry.

One of these roles is that of employee under contract of service, engaged to implement social policies, as formulated in legislation and its associated rules, regulations and circulars, and in the standing orders of local councils; and as interpreted locally, by, for example, Social Services Committees and Probation Committees. A second is the role of the professional who assumes individual responsibility for providing the best possible service to clients on the basis of professional criteria. A third may be that of a member of a professional association which corporately and legitimately undertakes pressure group activity to initiate or support moves which are intended to culminate in social reform, and may influence the shape legislation takes. A fourth is that of private citizen, whether as ratepayer, and a member of the public from which the sponsorship of statutory social services derives, or as political activist. Different behaviour is appropriate to and practicable within each of these roles even though the roles themselves cannot be neatly separated off from each other. There will not be universal agreement about either what is appropriate or what is practicable in any of them, but it is at least possible to offer some generalisations.

The first two roles (those of employee and professional individual) are implemented with the employing organisation constituting a major influence upon action, and both the possible conflicts between them and the potentialities of them are a main theme of this book, and will be referred to specifically at many points within it. At this stage, it may simply be said that although the emphasis so far has been placed on the public, rather than the professional, accountability and responsibility of social workers in statutory services, they are after all employed with the general intention that their professional knowledge and skills shall contribute to the provision of the best possible service. Herein is to be found an unequivocal justification for attempts by social workers to bring professional points of view to bear upon their employers: a matter which is central to the process of public administration, as discussed on pp. 44–9, and of professionalism as an element within it.

In the third and fourth roles (those of member of a professional association and of citizen), social workers have scope for active participation of the kind which is open to other professional groups and to citizens in general, in the political processes through which social sponsorship of public services is promulgated. The ways in which they implement these roles may be modified by their roles as employees of particular agencies: but their scope for attempting to influence public policy is not entirely bounded by their personal employment situation. At the same time, if much current confusion about the status and identity of social work derives from the impact of bureaucratic influences upon it, much can also be attributed both to the breakdown of traditional commitments to professionalism, and to the difficulties of reconciling political activism with both professionalism and with the role of public employee.

The problems involved in attempting to reconcile conflicting roles within publicly sponsored services can serve as a reminder that social services, like other social institutions, including social work, are best to be understood both as processes and as open systems. Social policy incorporates processes of continuous change in a changing society and the formal organisations through which publicly sponsored services are implemented cannot be tidily separated off from other systems with which they interact. Nor can the role of the social worker ever be defined exclusively by social workers. The cords which tie social work to the network of social processes and systems through which statutory social services are sponsored, developed and maintained, can never be cut.

To sum up, we may draw upon Titmuss's suggestion that 'all collectively provided services are deliberately designed to meet certain socially recognised needs: they are manifestations first of society's will to survive as an organic whole, and secondly of the expressed will of all the people to assist the survival of some people'.[3] This suggestion stresses the idea that the needs intended to be met through the social services are such as have been publicly recognised (although public understanding of them may be very limited) and it also implies that they are themselves societal as well as individual. However, public sponsorship of particular social services clearly does not mean that there has been or ever can be universal agreement on social policy, or on the forms which social services should take. It is more realistic to assume that such services are squarely in the middle of controversy to do with incompatible values. The situation in which social workers in such services find themselves may be described as one in which 'the belief that some single formula can in principle be found whereby all the diverse ends of men can be harmoniously realised, is demonstrably false'.[4]

Public financing

Public sponsorship of social services carries with it the public provision of financial resources for their maintenance and development. To describe at all specifically the diverse ways in which social services are or could be publicly financed is beyond both the scope and the intentions of this book. Several general points may however be made which seem particularly relevant to the social worker's implementation of his role, either within his own organisation, or in relation to other services whose assistance he seeks on behalf of his clients.

To begin with, there is the fact that the public financing of social services implies that the allocation of resources to them is an expression of public intent, whether at central or local government level. The origins of public financing are, like the legislative process itself, essentially a political activity, having to do with decisions made by the community's elected representatives or appointees, about how money is to be publicly recruited and deployed in pursuit of social objectives.

A second and associated point is that particular methods of financing social services are themselves instruments of social policy. Resources for particular services may be recruited from, for example, poll taxes on individuals or employers, from general taxation, from payments by individual users of particular services, from local rates, and so on. Some services may be financed nationally and entirely out of central exchequer funds, and others locally through a variety of combinations from the central exchequer and from rates. The diversity of methods available seems almost limitless. Each method has its own distinctive origins and significance, and serves particular political as well as social purposes, which may or may not be directly congruous with those which one would attribute to a particular social service.

Sometimes the methods by which a service is financed may be very clearly related to the explicit intentions of the social legislation by which the service was established. One of the most unequivocal examples of this was the shift from local to central exchequer financing in the National Assistance Act (1948), as an intrinsic part of the intention to create a truly national scheme of assistance removed from the sphere of local politics. On the other hand, the public financing of social services is not a self-contained process. It is open to the influence of both economic and political factors which are of much wider significance than the provision of particular services to individuals. Thus political decisions to expand capital expenditure on hospital building programmes may be taken on primarily economic grounds; the place of occupational pension schemes within a national retirement pension scheme is of economic and political as well as social significance, in that it affects the balance between the private and public sectors of the economy; and the methods by which the personal social services of local authorities are funded are a by-product of fundamental relationships between central and local government which extend throughout the whole sphere of Local Authority activity, and were certainly not devised specifically for social services. Like other services provided by Local Authorities, social services have at different times been financed both on a 'fifty-fifty' basis, and out of a block grant; and any future decisions on local government financing (such as modifications of the rating system) would affect them too. The methods by which social services are financed, no less than their public sponsorship, illustrate yet again that social services are best to be regarded as open systems, which can be understood only if their inter-connections with other and wider systems (such as local government, or the market system), are identified and acknowledged.

When the nature of administration comes to be considered, it will be suggested that it is basically to do with the recruitment and allocation of scarce resources in the face of perennially competing demands upon them. This is a problem at any level of social policy-making or implementation, nationally and within the local government system, as well as within individual organisations. Social services compete with other demands on publicly owned resources, and also with each other; and there is no guarantee that legislation which gives formal expression to the recognition of certain needs, will include financial provision for meeting those needs as they are perceived either by legislators, or by members of Local Authorities, or by those who are directly employed to implement the services concerned. The situation is further complicated by the fact that although the processes through which resources are allocated to particular services are essentially political, they are not identical with those through which legislation is enacted or amended. The 'community care' sections of the Mental Health Act (1959) provide an illustration. The relevant clauses of the Act may be said to have represented public sponsorship at national level of the 'idea' of community care; but the allocation of funds for the development of community care services was left very much to the discretion of individual Local Authorities. The re-organisation of the National Health Service in 1974, on the other hand, extended the scope of centralised and national financing and opened up the possibility of a more equitable distribution of nationally owned resources. This however was partly at the expense of local decision-making through the local government system. Here the value of equality of access to particular services, as an outcome of the more equitable distribution of nationally owned resources, is in conflict with values attaching to local decision-making by locally elected and accountable representatives.

If value-conflict in decisions about the deployment of scarce resources is one major feature of the public financing of social services, another crucial factor is the formal distribution of power throughout the political system. An example of specifically administrative significance is the committee structure of Local Authorities. Both the Children Act (1948) and the Local Authority Social Services Act (1970), which required the appointment of new kinds of chief officers and the establishment of new kinds of committee, represented attempts to secure power for those locally responsible for the services concerned: including the power to compete strongly within the Local Authority for resources for the implementation of the particular statutory functions delegated to them.

Finally, one must identify the problematic issue of discretion in the deployment of public moneys, both within particular services and between them. Social legislation embodies wide variations in the amount of discretion allowed to political and administrative systems in this respect. The social insurance legislation allows for practically no discretion in its day-to-day administration, while the Supplementary Benefits scheme has a discretionary element intentionally built into it. Some parts of the legislation implemented by Local Authorities are mandatory and also very specific, and funds must therefore be allocated to them. Other provisions are permissive, so that the discretion whether or not to finance them at all, and if so to what extent, rests with individual authorities. There are, however, also very extensive 'grey areas', where the provision of a service is mandatory, but where the interpretation of what this means in real terms, and of the financial backing which it should receive, is very much a discretionary matter. In the last resort and within limits and expectations of national policies, it is the council, advised by the committee which deals with its finances, which decides on the allocation of money to the Social Services Committee, which is competing with all the others. Furthermore, within a Social Services Committee itself, priorities have to be decided in the competition for resources between a Community Home, an Old People's Home, or a Day Centre for the mentally handicapped and so on. Although committees depend upon professional advice and information in using their discretion, as social workers will argue that they should, the authority to make submissions to the council in the form of a budget is vested in a committee of elected representatives, and not in an officer.

Throughout the whole process of administering and developing publicly sponsored services runs the problem of where the authority to make particular decisions should be located: in the political, or in the managerial or technical or professional parts of the system, and at what levels. Titmuss has suggested that one area of interest for the student of social policy and social services is the study of the role of government, local and central, as an 'allocator of rights to social property'.[5] The financing of statutory social services is one dimension of this role. It can be argued that those who are employed within the statutory social services are variously endowed with an authority to deploy resources which does not 'belong' to them as of right, but which has been delegated to them. By virtue of their particular technical and professional expertise, their role may properly, and intentionally, be both advisory and executive; but the resources which they participate in using or in allocating are in public ownership.

Public control

A corollary of the public sponsorship of statutory social services, and an accompaniment of public financing, are a variety of methods of public control. Before these are discussed, it is necessary to point to a distinction between 'public' control and 'social' control. Public control is here taken to mean control over the implementation and development of social services exercised through the formal structure and processes of government, either central or local. Public control is thus only one form of social control, which is itself much more varied in its manifestations, which may be much less formal and much more difficult to specify.

Although the emphasis here is to be on those forms of social control which are 'public', one point must be made about the concept of social control in general. The idea of social control, including by implication its public forms, tends to be regarded distastefully by social workers, in so far as it is considered to imply repressive action taken by or on behalf of a powerful elite to control the 'undesirable' behaviour of others. It may be worthwhile to emphasise, therefore, that the *concept* of social control is essentially neutral, and that it is particular forms of social control, and the purposes they are intended to serve, which may be deemed good or bad, on the basis of one's own value judgments. Thus, for example, social control may take the form of legislation designed to ensure the more equitable distribution of medical skills, or to require Local Authorities to provide certain services for the old or the handicapped, or to make provision for the training of social workers and the development of social work services. Indeed the existence of any social service may be said to imply forms of social control over the deployment of resources and over the operation of a market system. Any or all of such provisions may be judged desirable or not, or good in some ways and not in others. The idea of the 'coercive' social worker as an agent of repressive social control incorporates only one small part of the picture,[6] of which the public recruitment of resources to meet particular needs is another.

We may now consider some of the public controls which affect the structure and operation of the organisations within which social workers are employed.

Legislation itself not only provides sanctions for the implementation of particular services, but also sets limits to the range of services which are to be made available, and to the purposes for which public money may be spent. Additionally, the statutory rules and regulations by which Acts of Parliament are accompanied impose duties upon those whose responsibility it is to implement a service, and set limits to their discretion. A clear-cut example is the Adoption and Boarding Out Rules through which public control is exercised over the ways in which social workers implement what they themselves may wish to view as essentially professional roles. The pressure from a variety of sources in 1974-5 for a new Children Act was a recent example of the public expression of concern that arrangements for the public control of certain provisions for the care and protection of children, should be modified and in certain respects extended. Commenting on this, Robert Holman made the point that 'whereas the social work profession strongly pressed for the reforms of 1963, 1969 and 1970, present pressures for child care legislation are from other sources'.[7] Some of the pressures took the form of demands for extended legal or judicial controls over the activities of social workers.

The specificity of formal controls clearly varies from service to service, and even within particular pieces of legislation. Thus, for example, some clauses of the Children Act (1948) are much more specifically supported by statutory rules than are others. Alongside those in which the duties of Local Authorities are spelled out in detail, are others the interpretation of which allows for considerable latitude;

as that in which 'where a child is in the care of a Local Authority, it shall be the duty of that authority to exercise their powers with respect to him so as to further his best interests, and to afford him the opportunity for the proper development of his character and abilities'.[8] One always interesting question is whether the degree and extent of public control exercised in formal ways such as those mentioned so far, is appropriate to the implementation of the kind of service which Parliament has intended to sponsor. Is the control sufficiently flexible to allow for the provision of a personal service to individuals? Is it sufficiently close to protect citizens from unintended uses of professional or administrative discretion?

Whatever the original intentions, Acts of Parliament are less dynamic than the situations in which the social services based upon them are implemented, and the public controls embodied in legislation change in significance and relevance as time goes by. Thus the original requirement of the Children Act (1948) that Local Authorities should place a child in a Home only if it was not practicable or desirable to board him out, might be said to have constituted a form of control over the actions of social workers which was to become less appropriate over time, as professional knowledge and skills were developed within the Child Care service itself.

Reference to the roles of Local Authorities in the implementation of social services has so far been concentrated upon their statutory duties in respect of national policies. On the other hand, the activities of councils and their committees, as bodies of elected representatives of local constituencies, also constitute a form of public control over policy development and implementation within their own areas. Councillors are constitutionally responsible to the electorate for the ways in which publicly owned resources are deployed; and chief officers are formally accountable to the Local Authority. The National Health Service Reorganisation Act (1973) on the other hand, at least in so far as the services formerly provided by Local Authorities are concerned, may be said to have provided for the creation of a structure from which the very concept of public control at local level is absent. The Area Health Authorities control no resources for the provision of services, have no executive authority, and are not elected but appointed. In contrast, the Local Authority Social Services Act (1970) provided for the establishment of a formal structure in which an executive officer, the Director of Social Services, is immediately accountable to a committee composed of elected representatives of a local constituency.

Even where such formal machinery of control exists, however, one of the most crucial problems of social policy and indeed of democratic government, may be the lack of vitality of a system in which links between councillors and citizens are weak, and inadequate to sustain communication on the local issues by which people's lives are affected.

Partly because of public apathy, and partly because power has increasingly passed from elected representatives to the 'experts' whom they employ, public control may extensively be more myth than reality.[9]

Nevertheless, the organisational structures through which statutory social services are administered, and in which social workers are employed, constitute formal accountability systems through which varying degrees and types of public control are exercised over the activities carried on within them. These organisations, however, are neither closed systems nor perfect ones. As has been illustrated above, discretion is intentionally left to the administrators and professionals who hold positions within the formal structure; but the holders of such positions may in practice assume for themselves discretion for which there is no legitimation other than that which they themselves ascribe to professional standards, or in the exercise of which personal value judgments predominate.

One specifically problematic area is that of public control over the deployment of public funds. Questions have continually to be asked both about where the power to control the use of public funds really lies, and where it ought to lie. What kind of balance is there in specific instances, and what kind ought there to be, between the administrative control of resources (in which professionals may play an active part) on the one hand, and public control on the other? What control should rest with committees, and what should be delegated throughout the formal structure of a department? And by what criteria may one judge whether or not the balance is a good one?

So far, public control has been presented as finding expression in the forms taken by legislation, in the administrative or organisational structures through which social services are implemented, and through the activities of elected representatives, including those which have to do with the allocation of publicly owned resources. A less formal element, and one which is more accurately described as 'social' or 'political' rather than 'public', must now at least be identified: the lobby.

Finer defines the lobby as 'the sum of organisations in so far as they are occupied at any point in time in trying to influence the policy of public bodies in their own chosen direction'.[10] He concludes that 'the advantages of having a profusion of private associations to check and balance and advise and warn the public authorities are very obvious'.[11]

The control over policy developments which is exerted through pressure group activity is a form of social control in that it is the outcome of a situation in which individuals sharing common attitudes or interests organise themselves to promote shared objectives. It is clearly different from forms of social control which are public in the sense that they emanate, at least in theory, from 'the people as a whole' via their elected representatives. However, at one end of a continuum of relationships, contact between pressure groups and 'Westminster' and 'Whitehall' is of so sustained and institutionalised a kind, that Finer goes so far as to suggest that 'for better or for worse, such self government as we now enjoy today is one that operates by and through the lobby'.[12]

In contrast to this kind of pressure group activity, and at the other end of a continuum, may be placed the relationship to representative government of a type of activity not even identified by Finer in 1966: that of grassroots activist groups of which the objectives include greater direct participation in and control of policy and planning developments, in a situation in which the system of representative government itself is deemed to be ineffective. Backing for greater community participation is to be found in both the Skeffington[13] and Seebohm[14] reports; and Geoff Green suggests that 'there are no overriding reasons why local community activity of this kind should not slot into the representative system'.[15] This, however, presupposes that councillors are both willing and able to maintain a balanced response to the needs or demands expressed by activist groups on the one hand, and to the needs of the local government area as a whole on the other. For social workers who are employed in local government, sensitivity or commitment to this particular form of social control over policy developments must give rise to problems, as such social workers are increasingly exposed to, or increasingly encourage, the maximum participation of individuals and groups in the community in the planning, organisation, and provision of the social services.[16] Who are social workers in local government there to serve: the organisational hierarchy, the local councillors, the public at large, the most forceful groups within that public, or groups which they themselves identify as in need of support or protection? To whom are such social workers accountable; and to whom should they be?

The extent to which, and the ways in which public and other controls are exercised over both the development and the implementation of social services are matters of social fact which impinge directly upon the ways in which social workers implement their professional roles, and which they therefore need to understand as fully as they can. At the same time, such controls may be viewed as social facts which continuously call for value judgments by social workers, who have to attempt to reconcile their roles as private citizens, professional persons, and employees. Specifically, the extension of social control through direct citizen participation in local planning, may increasingly expose social workers to situations in which value judgments on the conflicting demands of different groups cannot be avoided and in which a politically neutral stance may be difficult to hold. The Acts of Parliament, the rules and regulations, the committees of elected representatives and so on, which constitute formal systems of public control over the behaviour of administrators and social workers, also afford some protection to them. The extension of social control through direct citizen participation in local planning, desirable though it may be believed to be, affords no such protection.

The range of methods of public control over the development and operation of statutory social services is much more extensive that the systems referred to here. It includes such institutions as standing Advisory Councils; the formal enquiries which may be set up by Ministers or by Parliament when things go patently wrong; the administrative tribunals which are intended to act as checks upon the maladministration of services; and so on. It is also perhaps worth while for social workers to reflect that although the CCETSW, which carries statutory authority to promote training in all fields of social work, is staffed by professional social workers, it is not itself a professional body. It is a public one upon which both central government and employing bodies, as well as professional interests, are strongly represented.

Public administration

The discussion of statutory social services so far has been intended to stress the point that the roles which social workers carry cannot be adequately understood if they are considered as simply 'professional', without reference to the extra-professional influences upon them which accompany public sponsorship, financing and control. It now remains to consider the significance of the public nature of social services for the administrative process itself.

No discussion of public administration is possible without a preliminary distinction being made between the political sector (the government, Parliament, the Local Authority) and the administrative one (departments of central and local government). For the moment (but see chapter 4) administrators are taken to include all those who are employed in such departments to implement services which the political parts of the system sanction.

Administration is a generic process in the sense that no formal organisation of any kind is possible without it; and considerable emphasis will later (see chapter 4) be placed on elements which are common to it whatever type of organisation is in question. On the other hand, as public sponsorship, financing, and control are features of statutory social services, so their administration is also of a 'public' as distinct from a 'private' kind.[17] Publicly owned, such services are 'run' by departments of central and local government or, as in the case of the Probation and After-Care Service, as part of the organisation of the courts of law. The roles of those who administer social services are consequentially defined not only by whatever may be their personal commitments to social welfare, or to the professional objectives of social work, but by the positions which they hold in organisations which are not simply social work agencies, or even self-contained organisations, but part of a network of formal structures established for the public administration of politically sanctioned services. Illustrations of the administrative significance of this situation, within the frame-work of public sponsorship, financing, and control, may be drawn from local government.

First, it is suggested, a core problem is that of 'clarifying the meaning of management within the political context'.[18] The Maud Committee on the management of local government suggested that 'the management and execution of governmental functions, as opposed to those of industry and commerce, are made more difficult to organise because two sets of people are involved: the members and the officers'.[19] As departments of local government have come to be headed and staffed by 'experts', it is no longer useful to operate on the assumption that it is the function of elected representatives to formulate policy, and of the officers to carry it out. It is rational for elected representatives to draw on the expertise of their chief officers, for this is why they have appointed them. Similarly, it is reasonable for such officers to take the view that if their specialist advice is not incorporated into the policy-making activities of their employers, their time and skills are being wasted.

As John Stuart Mill suggested was the case with representative government, political machinery does not act of itself: 'as it is first made, so it must be worked — by men, and even by ordinary men. It needs not their simple acquiescence, but their active participation, and must be adjusted to the capacities and qualities of such men as are available'.[20] A century later we are confronted with a situation in which it seems that 'ordinary men', as elected representatives, are becoming increasingly dependent upon 'experts', and in which 'the "is" question about what administrators or politicians do is intimately bound up with the "ought" question about what they should do'.[21] How are the roles of elected representatives and officers defined in practice, and how ought they to be defined, in a system of representative government in which employees are experts in their own fields, but of which the democratic intention requires that the powers of experts be held in check by 'ordinary men'? The system itself may be at risk in situations in which elected representatives feel themselves to be lost, and unable to exercise independent judgment, in a world of technical expertise and of the esoteric knowledge to which profes-sionals lay claim. Furthermore, where decisions have to be reached not only about what can be done, but about what ought to be done, is one to assume that the values of experts (such as architects or town planners or social workers) should be accorded priority over those of 'ordinary men'? 'Expertise' may conflict with the 'conventional wisdom', or with what experts might describe as the prejudices of laymen, and values incorporated into professional practice may run counter to those which are dominant in lay committees. While professionals may legitimately seek to justify their own interpretations of situations, the reverse side of the question has to do with the ways in which, and the extent to which, it is desirable that social life should be shaped by experts (managers, planners, technologists, professionals, and so on), rather than by those who, however imperfectly the system works, have been elected to represent their constituents.

The complexities of the situation become more visible if one takes the view, as did the Maud Committee,[22] that 'policy' and 'administration' are not two distinct processes, but interact continuously with each other. In so far as this is the case, it would seem that policy-making cannot be assigned to one part of the system and administration to the other, and that the operation of a Local Authority requires co-operative activity by elected representatives and officers, according to the requirements of specific situations, rather than a formal allocation of functions to one or the other element. Peter Self argues that, in any case, a clear definition of the policy and the technical aspects of operations is ethically undesirable: 'we should think rather poorly of an education officer or a town planning officer who regarded the policies he was implementing as not his concern, and we would be equally critical of a councillor who was unconcerned with the treatment of junior staff, or with the detailed line of a new road'.[23]

Self would assign to councillors the task of exercising a review power over the substantial and growing professional discretion exercised by officers, adding that the activities of councillors themselves may need to be balanced by some form of functional or consumer representation.[24] The relevance of such controversial issues derives from the essentially political nature of the context within which the services provided by Local Authorities are implemented and developed, and without reference to which the roles of public administrators cannot be defined.

The second illustration has to do with accountability. Even though chief officers may properly advise lay committees, and in practice influence them, it remains a fact that they are employed to act on a committee's behalf. The term 'agency', although not in an exclusively social work sense, describes quite precisely one important feature of the departments which they head: 'the very word "agency" implies the presence of some person or people on whose behalf the agency acts'.[25] Social workers will tend to take the view that the agency is there to act on behalf of clients. Another interpretation is that it acts on behalf of the Local Authority. The authority vested in chief officers is delegated to them by their employers, or is legally attached to the positions which they hold, and they are ultimately accountable for what they do with it. The concept of accountability will be explored more specifically later (pp. 103–4), but in relation to public administration as such, reference must be made here to its effect upon chief officers. They must be able, if necessary, to justify retrospectively decisions which they themselves have taken, or which have been taken by members of their departments to whom they in their turn have delegated authority. Whatever form the internal structure of a department of local government may take, it has constitutionally to be one in which accountability is centred in the office-holder at the apex of it. For political as well as for organisational or managerial reasons a formal hierarchy in which accountability is concentrated, may be a necessary component of such a structure: although this is not to say that such a hierarchy need be an extended one.

Third, departments of local government, as has been suggested already, are not self-contained organisations, and the nature of what goes on at their boundaries – at their points of contact with their environment – is a further determinant of the ways in which they have to be administered. Hill suggests that 'it is the organisation's relationships with its environment that are fundamental to its existence, and in the case of public administration . . . this means that politics is of fundamental importance'.[26]

At the boundaries of any department of local government are the individual councillors, the committees, the council, members of the general public, and the local lobby, all of whose activities combine to constitute local politics. There is also a network of the other departments of local government with which interaction is inescapable, either because of dependency upon the services which they provide, or because they are the source of a variety of controls on matters in which uniform policies or practices operate throughout the whole range of the authority's jurisdiction. There are also the numerous and varied organisations external to the Local Authority itself with which, because of the nature of their respective functions, departments of local government must enter into relationships of interaction and exchange.

Moreover, such external influences are not exclusively local. There are departments of central government which exercise control at Local Authority level, in a variety of ways, including the issue of 'policy' circulars, requests for information, requirements that long-term plans be drawn up, and control over resources. Indeed, one view of local government sees it as 'an administrative device for the provision of national services . . . in which the relation between the local authority and central government is that of agent and principal'.[27] Even if the relationship is perceived predominantly as a partnership, there are very specific ways, as well as more intangible ones, in which departments of

47

local government are either affected by, or required to implement, national policy. In any case, they may legally act only within the framework of duties or powers which have been conferred upon them by Parliament. Both resources and restraints originate extensively from outside any individual department, and this means that the concern of a chief officer in local government must be as much with the environment of the department of which he is head as with what goes on inside it. The point may be illustrated by two examples.

The first example has to do with goals. In industry, there will be at least a general consensus between boards of directors and management about the overriding objective of the enterprise: to stay in business at a profit. In local government, there can be no such consensus, either within the council itself, or between council and committees, between committees and chief officers, or between chief officers themselves. For one thing, the 'enterprise' which is local government is constituted of too many and heterogeneous activities. The very general and imprecise goal of improved services has to coexist within councils with that of 'keeping down the rates'; and in no case is a chief officer at the head of a department or service the expansion of which is the primary goal of the body which owns the resources upon which expansion depends.

The second example is the concept of chief officers not simply as heading particular departments, but as members of a management team. In the opinion of the Maud committee, 'the separateness of the committees contributes to the separateness of departments, and the professionalism of departmental staff feeds on this separateness'.[28] Controversial though the notion of corporate planning may be,[29] the roles of chief officers are already being modified by it. For example, the *primus inter pares* role of the clerk to the council is being replaced by one into which is incorporated an element of managerial authority over heads of individual departments, the principals amongst whom may also act as members of the Local Authority's management team. To the extent that policies and structures aimed at combating the separateness of departments and of committees develop, the notion of self-contained and autonomous departments will become even less meaningful than it is at present. In any case, although a chief officer 'heads' a department, he is not autonomous, but accountable to his employers who are not members of that department, and whose goals cannot be identical with those which he might wish to adopt. The interconnectedness of the different parts of the whole local government system becomes increasingly apparent if one looks at the structure of committee membership, and remembers that councillors have multiple roles to carry within the council. If one thinks of the chairman of the Social Services Committee, for example, as also a member of the council's major policy committee, and possibly of other committees which compete with social services for resources, it is possible to realise that he cannot look at situations from an exclusively 'social services' angle.

In all these ways, the departments implementing the services provided by local councils are linked to an outside world, and shaped by what goes on at their boundaries. They have no identity except as part of both the administrative and the political systems of government, and their nature begins to be comprehensible only if these aspects of their environment are reckoned with.

To sum up, public administration in local government is both an organisational and a political kind of activity, in which elected representatives and those who administer the services are mutually engaged. Additionally, and in spite of a specifically different set of factors from those which apply in local government, the probation service, as the other major statutory service within which social workers are employed, is no less 'public'.

The Bains working party on Local Authority management and structure points to what is perhaps the main implication of the 'public' nature of the type of administration which is intrinsic to the implementation of statutory social services. It emphasises that in a democratic institution such as local government, administrative criteria of efficiency cannot be the only consideration.[30] Those who are employed to administer such services, are accorded status and authority in order that they may act as instruments of publicly (as distinct from administratively or professionally) intended ends, and it is within such limits that both administrative and professional roles have to be constructed and implemented.

Professionalism in publicly administered social services

Statutory social services have been described as publicly sponsored, financed, and controlled, and as publicly administered in so far as both representatives of the public and salaried staff share in their administration, with the latter being ultimately accountable to the former. The illustrations given here of the nature of public administration have been drawn from local government, and major differences between the organisation of Local Authority services, the income maintenance schemes, the Probation and Aftercare Service, and the NHS are not far to seek. Nevertheless, the problem of achieving proper balances between the roles of unpaid and part-time committee or board members on the one hand, and paid administrators on the other, is common to them all. A very specific example is to be found in the restructured NHS. Since the reorganisation of 1974, there has been no structure of accountability of paid staff of the service to a local electorate, and the councils established at both area and regional levels are advisory and not policy-making bodies. It could be argued that the service is to this extent less democratically administered than was previously the case, and that the government which legislated for the change gave the objective of administrative efficiency priority over local democracy.

If, however, the public, and indeed the essentially political, nature of statutory services exerts such an influence on administrative structures and processes as to mean that public administration is significantly different from the administration of other types of institutions, may the same be said in the case of professionalism in public services? The idea was discussed in chapter 1 that employment in any formal organisation modifies the nature of professional activity, and we may now consider how the *public* nature of any organisation either is or should be a significant factor in the ways in which professional roles are implemented.

Within whatever part of the public services they work, professional people both as individuals and as members of professional associations, seek both to define their roles for themselves and to extend their professional power. Public policy on the other hand also contributes to the definition of professional roles in a variety of ways: by imposing duties upon professionals and by setting limits to what they may do, and additionally by providing them (also within limits) with resources, and with discretion to act as their professional judgment decrees. However, and perhaps most significantly, professionals are employed in public services because their knowledge and skills are required for the implementation of public policy. Stated bluntly, this means that they are employed to serve public purposes, and that the public does not assume that all wisdom will die with them. The point is put less crudely by Alwyn Roberts: 'the notion of professionalism operates within the context of socially agreed and commonly understood ends. Within such a context professional freedom and authority are granted subject to these aims and ends. The professional is accorded status and freedom in that he is seen to be the servant and necessary instrument for their achievement.'[3][1]

Examples of the consequential tensions between public policy and professional aspirations may be drawn both from medicine, and from the much less powerful and less clearly defined occupation of social work.

The history of the NHS has included the process of incorporating into a public service professionals one of whose continuing concerns has been to protect their professional autonomy. The political issues to be faced in 1945 as soon as the government had decided to introduce legislation have been summarised and commented upon by Eckstein:[3][2]

What should be the profession's role in the drafting of actual legislation? Should it be allowed to 'negotiate' with the Minister, or should

it merely be allowed to 'discuss'? Should it be in a position actually to approve or reject legislation, or should it merely be permitted to voice its viewpoint and furnish expert knowledge in consultation?

This was not a simple issue to resolve, even though constitutional doctrine may be quite clear on the point. Constitutionally, legislation is a parliamentary and Cabinet function, not a matter of haggling between the Ministries and the social groups affected bv it.

The implementation of the NHS required the participation of the medical profession, and the forces of constitutional propriety and of professional power are not easily distinguishable from each other during the formative period of the legislation: even although Aneurin Bevan as Minister of Health stood by the view that whereas 'discussion' was acceptable, 'negotiation' was not. Our main concern here, however, is not to explore the influence of a particular profession upon the creation and development of a particular social service, but only to illustrate the existence of situations in which 'public' and 'professional' interests interact and may conflict, and to suggest that there may sometimes be a case for giving priority to the former.

In short, throughout the history of the NHS, concern for clinical freedom on the part of both doctors and governments has co-existed with ideas about the extent to which and the ways in which professional autonomy should be modified by public control. One specific issue surfaced in 1974, when the government declared a policy of phasing out private practice from the NHS. For some members of the medical profession, this will have the effect of modifying if not the scope of clinical freedom itself, at least the type of situation in which it is exercised.

A move of a kind which effectively extends professional discretion, both within the NHS and outside it, was included in the Abortion Act (1968): 'the clinical assessment of the desirability of abortion or the technique necessary to perform the operation was not altered by the Act. The legislation simply enlarged the field in which unfettered clinical decisions might be made. After a policy decision had been taken, questions which had been public and political became professional'.[33] This particular change in the law relating to abortion, illustrates the use of legislation not to restrict the freedom of professional practitioners, but rather to extend it. Nevertheless it remains the case that the circumstances in which a doctor is 'free' to perform an abortion operation are still defined by the law: the discretion is not his by right as a member of a profession, but has been delegated to him. At the same time, this change in the law may gradually alter the freedom of doctors not to perform such operations, in so far as it modifies the expectations of would-be patients, and the demands which they make upon doctors.

51

Both abortion law reform and the controversy about the status of private practice within the NHS illustrate that even in the most highly professionalised occupation of medicine, unlimited professional freedom is modified by public policy. And how many social workers are there who would argue that it should not be?

As far as Local Authority Social Services Departments are concerned, the public control of professional activity has been described as having produced a situation in which there cannot be said to be a 'defined and inviolable area which is the professional worker's own by right. Rather would it be realistic to say that social workers in such departments exercise discretion which has been delegated to them by those who are accountable for how it is then exercised'.[34] Social workers seem sometimes to assume that if only there were more of them in statutory social services, they would be able to 'get down to real social work' as they themselves would like to define it. A more realistic approach, however, might be to accept that 'real' social work has to be defined in relation to the circumstances in which social workers find themselves: it is not of a kind which it is at the discretion of the profession itself to determine without reference to the essentially public nature of the situations in which social workers are employed.

Such an interpretation of the status and nature of social work in public services may seem to be depressingly deterministic. If social work roles are so extensively publicly determined, and if professional values are not to be accorded unquestioned priority over those of laymen, can professional social work be said to have an identity to call its own? The balance may be redressed by emphasising once again that one reason for the public employment of social workers is that at least something of their 'way of working' for the welfare of their clients is publicly acknowledged and approved. Second, even if they cannot be said to have unlimited professional freedom, discretion is indeed delegated to them. Third, ways are open to them, individually and as members both of peer groups within their employing organisations and of their professional associations, to promote their own professional purposes. Thus the situation of professionals in public services in general is not being presented as closed, but rather as one in which forces of an extra-professional kind require to be acknowledged as influences which are both significant and legitimate. The tension which accompanies the existence of professional concern for professional standards in public services, may be indicative of both the need for, and the possibility of, continuous modifications in a symbiotic relationship. Professionals may argue in all sincerity that their professional judgment is an adequate criterion for action in individual cases, or that their expert opinions should carry greater weight in relation to legislative reform. However, especially in situations where the value-element in professional decisions or opinions is particularly strong, unrestricted professional autonomy might be as socially unsatisfactory as would rigid political or bureaucratic control of professional behaviour. Public control and professional discretion together constitute a system of checks and balances, and in the case of social work it is not the existence of this system, but rather the nature of professional participation in it which should be seen as problematic.

Doctors may work in situations in which they believe that clinical freedom is being eroded by public policy of which the purpose is the more equitable distribution and deployment of medical skills. Social workers may believe on the basis of their own professional judgment that legislation intended to secure greater welfare of children may misfire. In so far as both doctors and social workers do their work within public services, their professional selves have to co-exist with the roles assigned to them as public servants. Their professional associations however can mobilise as pressure groups as and when they think fit to do so, and are free to attempt to modify the course which public policy takes.[35]

Examples of the situation confronting professional people in public services have so far been drawn exclusively from social work and from medicine. As, however, this book is essentially to do with administration, it may be relevant to make at least a brief reference at this point to problems of professional standards in the practice of administration itself. In the course of an attempt to define professional standards in the old administrative class of the civil service,[36] the suggestion was made that ethical problems encountered by civil servants are in no small part due to their constitutional position, in which they have multiple responsibilities: to a Minister, to the government, to the community at large, and to official colleagues and seniors; as well as to their own consciences. Concern at the lack of guiding standards in conflicting situations such as this, a desire for safeguards against organisational authoritarianism, and a wish to see closer investigation of governmental processes, reflect the idea that the role of the civil servant as a professional administrator cannot be summed up in terms of technical expertise and efficiency. He may be superficially described as a 'public servant': but how is the role of public servant to be defined in situations in which the 'public interest' cannot be objectively ascertained, and in which official duties may conflict with individual consciences? The dilemmas to which such situations give rise are not primarily to do with the internal organisational structure of the civil service, but derive rather from the political nature of the system within which the civil servant, or indeed the local government officer, is employed.

Some of the ways in which professional roles are modified by employment in organisations were discussed in chapter 1. To over-emphasise the impact of formal organisations upon professional practice in statutory social services without placing such organisations themselves in context, however, is to risk losing sight of another equally important influence: that of the publicly sponsored, financed, controlled and administered social service of which any 'agency' or 'department' or 'organisation' is only a part. Although social workers may tend to think of themselves primarily as implementing roles in which the dominant conflict is between their professional aspirations and what they believe to be their organisational situations, the fact that the formal organisations in which and from which they work are components of social services, must be recognised as influencing both organisational structure and administrative processes. No organisation or management theory which fails to take into account the public and political nature of social service organisations can provide an adequate basis from which to attempt to understand them. It may consequently be that social work roles in public services should be regarded as being essentially three-dimensional: professional, organisational and, in the broadest possible sense, political.

The voluntary sector

The essence of a voluntary social service is to be found in the fact of its being neither publicly sponsored nor publicly controlled, but both initiated and governed by its own members. Additionally, an ideal type model of a voluntary social service might incorporate the attributes of non-governmental financing; of functions, purposes and philosophies of which the sanctions are other than legislative; and of freedom from public accountability. Voluntary organisations providing services, as distinct from those acting exclusively as pressure groups, may be broadly categorised into those which provide services for their own members (mutual aid) and those through which services are given to clients (philanthropy). Some of either type may approximate closely to the ideal type model. In practice, however, the voluntary services together constitute so heterogeneous a collection that differences amongst them must be given equal consideration with similarities. Voluntary services differ amongst each other in, for example, the scope and type of their activities, their scale, durability, sources of financial support, dependence upon voluntary workers, and constitutional form. Most importantly, taking the definitive factor of autonomy in initiation and government into account, they may also be said to vary extensively in their degree of 'voluntaryness'.

On the broad front of social service development, voluntary action in Britain has indeed been said to be 'part of public policy'.[37] Over a wide field, social legislation provides both for the active participation of voluntary agencies in the provision of services for which a Minister is ultimately responsible to Parliament, and for public control of certain of their activities, by such devices as requiring them to conform to statutory rules and regulations, and subjecting them to government inspection. Ministers, and even in one instance a Prime Minister,[38] have pronounced upon the part which they considered voluntary services should play in relation to the public sector; and in 1972 the government of the day went so far as to designate a Minister of State at the Home Office to assume special responsibility for co-ordinating the interest of the government in voluntary services.[39]

Very generally, the redefinition of the role of voluntary social services in the meeting of need may be said to be a permanent issue of public policy. The public and the voluntary sectors of social service provision cannot be meaningfully regarded as independent of each other: together they constitute the arena or, it might be said, the 'mixed economy' of social policy. As in the process of legislative reform policy decisions are taken concerning the role to be allocated to voluntary services, so in voluntary social services themselves, policy makers must keep one eye on what is happening in the public sector. By redefining its own sphere of activity, either central or local government may modify the scope of voluntary action, on the basis of ideas about the needs which it is considered should be met through the provision of public services, and about what should, or can, be left to voluntary agencies. The voluntary services themselves may respond either in advance or retrospectively to such modifications.

Moreover, the fundamental issues of what particular services government should provide and what should be left to voluntary provision apart, the policy problems in relation to which the two sectors interact are legion. For example, in what ways does the public interest require that the activities of voluntary agencies (such as the provision of residential care for children or for older people) be publicly controlled? To what extent and for what purposes should voluntary services be publicly financed? Is there anything to be said for public financing without public control? Such issues of public policy impinge upon the interests of the voluntary sector too. What may be the implications for a voluntary service of undertaking functions which are statutorily controlled? What may be the advantages and disadvantages of dependency upon government, central or local, for money? How ought a particular voluntary service, at a particular time, to modify its activities in the light of changes in statutory social service provision?

What we have in effect is not two separate systems, but a pattern of social provision in which 'public' and 'voluntary' are linked at a thousand points. Public involvement in the provision of social services is not confined to the statutory sector, and the public financing and control which have been discussed in earlier sections of this chapter in relation to statutory services, may extend to services which are meaningfully described as voluntary. Indeed (as Voluntary Service Overseas, the Young Volunteer Force, and the system of voluntary associates in the Probation and Aftercare Service illustrate), services which are in some respects voluntary may even be publicly sponsored or administered. A rational examination of the nature of any voluntary service must include an exploration of its formal relationship to the public sector, and of the ways in which its 'voluntaryness' is modified by this relationship. The combination of public with other forms of sponsorship, financing, control and administration, will be different from that which operates in statutory services; but except in the case of the most informal and ephemeral voluntary service, some combination is likely to be found. At one end of a continuum of formal relationships, some voluntary services may be so closely associated with statutory ones that they may be regarded, at least in some of their aspects, as ancillary to them, or as agents or extensions of them.

Some types of public intervention in the implementation and development of voluntary services have already been referred to incidentally, in illustration of the kinds of policy issue which are implicit in the formulation of relationships between the two sectors. All such intervention implies the existence of policy problems for them both; and with this in mind, some of the major forms which public control of voluntary services takes can now be categorised.

A beginning may be made with the Charities Act (1960), which requires that with certain exceptions and exemptions, charitable organisations in England and Wales must be registered with the Charity Commissioners who have power to institute enquiries into the activities of charities, whether registered or not. Although registration brings certain financial advantages, it may also present problems. For example, one very significant factor is the power given to the Commissioners to decide what constitutes charitable as distinct, for example, from political activity, and to take to task charities engaging in activities which appear to the Commissioners to be in breach of trust:[40]

> Many organisations now feel it is not sufficient simply to alleviate distress arising from particular social conditions . . . . They feel compelled also to draw attention as forcibly as possible to the needs which they think are not being met, to rouse the conscience of the public to demand action and to press for effective official provision to be made to meet those needs. . . . If trustees of a charity stray into the field of political activity their action will be in breach of trust and they could be called on at law to recoup to the charity any of its funds which have been spent outside its purposes.

The significance of this for charities which wish to engage in pressure group activity is not far to seek, and it would be difficult to find a clearer example of external restraints upon organisational activity.

Second, the legislation which constitutes the basis of statutory services, may also make provision for the active participation of voluntary agencies in the implementation of these services; require their conformity to certain statutory rules and regulations; and open them to inspection by departments of government. In addition to the provision of residential care for deprived children and for the old, which have been referred to already, examples would be voluntary adoption agencies, and certain services for the handicapped provided by voluntary agencies acting as agents of Local Authorities under the National Assistance Act (1948). As Murray points out, there are fields of social service provision in which voluntary services and Local Authorities carry out executive functions more or less together.[41]

Third, associated with public controls of such kinds as those just mentioned is public accountability. In many voluntary services, this may barely exist. On the other hand, in some spheres sanctions are available which may be used, although perhaps only in the last resort, against voluntary agencies defecting in their implementation of statutory functions. Such would be the case with voluntary Children's Homes which are regulated under the Children Act (1948). Additionally, agencies which receive financial assistance from either central or local government are in a competitive situation, in which they may have to demonstrate by their own performance that the continuation of such assistance is merited. In any case, the discretion to give or withhold such assistance is at the disposal of public bodies.

While considering that public accountability is in practice 'a very marginal proposition', Murray sees it as 'essentially a financial question'[42]; and financial arrangements may indeed be identified as a fourth illustration of the forms which public intervention and control may take. The general powers of public bodies to give or withhold financial assistance apart, voluntary services operate within the framework of certain specific legislative requirements to do with their financial management. For example, those which are registered as limited companies must have their accounts audited annually. On a very broad front, the significance of public policy for the general financial climate within which voluntary services may have to work, may perhaps be best illustrated by quoting at some length from the speech of the Prime Minister already referred to:[43]

> I expect, with some confidence, that local authorities will continue to make their own notable contribution towards local voluntary services. But I think we all recognise that a really healthy voluntary movement must be able to call on resources of its own. After all, that is probably the strongest guarantee of independence. Yet, here

too, the government has a part to play. It is to pursue the economic and tax objectives which will stimulate economic expansion and allow those who create that new national wealth to keep a reasonable share of it.

Taxation has an important part to play in this. . . . But in the end it is by our efforts as individuals, not as taxpayers, that our contribution to the social welfare of the nation will be judged.

Fifth, public control may be exercised through public representation on the governing bodies of voluntary services. Individual services may invite representatives of local government to membership of their committees: but the element of public control may be much stronger than this. An example is to be found in the Children and Young Persons Act (1969), which empowers the Secretary of State to make instruments of management providing for the constitution of a body of management for any voluntary Home incorporated into a regional plan, and specifying the percentage of members to be appointed by the Local Authority.[44] In such cases, the actual constitutional structure of a voluntary organisation is statutorily determined.

So far, this discussion of the features of voluntary services which influence their organisational structures and processes, has concentrated on the ways in which such services are subject to public intervention. Public sponsorship, financing, control and administration have been illustrated as spilling over from the public to the voluntary sector and, more specifically, public control has been categorised as taking the form of legal requirements concerning registration, statutory allocations of functions, regulation of day-to-day operation, elements of public accountability, sanctions associated with public financing and, in certain cases, statutory control of constitutional structure. What has been said indeed lends support to T. H. Marshall's view that the differences between statutory and voluntary services are not as great as is commonly supposed.[45] On the other hand, it has been stressed both that the very essence of a voluntary service lies in its autonomy from public intervention, and that such services vary considerably in their degree of voluntaryness. If public intervention is a factor to be reckoned with, so also are social factors of a 'non-public' kind: and to the extent that a service is truly voluntary, it will be dependent upon and influenced by social factors of a 'private' rather than a public nature.

In the voluntary sector, however, no less than in the public, what goes on in individual organisations, as well as something of what one might think ought to go on, is affected by the nature of the service of which any one particular organisation is only a part. Although the frame of reference is different, the concepts of sponsorship, financing, control and accountability, and the species of administration, discussed in relation to statutory services, are of equal relevance to an analysis of the ways in which the nature of a voluntary service affects the structure and processes of the formal organisations through which it is implemented.

Conceptual similarities, together with some identification of differences in application, can be illustrated by a brief reference to control and accountability. A general concept relevant to the analysis of the formal structure of public social services is that of the constitutional responsibility of those who administer them to those on whose behalf they are administered. It is the *public* nature of the personal social services of local authorities which generates formal organisations incorporating accountability systems at the head of which are directors who are formally accountable to committees of elected representatives, which themselves both exercise control on behalf of a local constituency, and are sub-units of a system of which the provision of social services is only one of many functions. But what of the truly voluntary social service, which is by definition self-governing and to that extent self-controlling? In such a service there is no formal accountability to an external constituency; there are no externally imposed obligations to clients; and the ideal type voluntary agency, unlike the statutory one, is free from controls of the kind which accompany existence as part of wider organisational systems such as those of local government. All these are factors which can influence both the ways in which such agencies are administered and structured, and the nature of working relationships within them.

For example, the absence of responsibility for the implementation of statutory functions modifies both the need for a formal accountability structure from social worker to employer, and the kind of control which a committee may need to exercise in relation to the heads of agencies. Formally, the governing body of a voluntary service which conforms closely to the ideal type model, may be accountable only to itself, and in the absence of formal external sanctions, normative sanctions may be more important than the structuring of formal systems of accountability. To whom, however, should the governing body of a voluntary service consider itself morally responsible? To its members? To its clients, who (as distinct from members of mutual aid societies) have no formal rights as beneficiaries, and no constitutional representatives? To those who provide it with money (supposing that it knows who they are)? To a body (such as a church) under whose broad umbrella it was established?

With this brief reference to control and accountability as an example, it is again emphasised that although the forms which they take and the questions to which they give rise will differ, the major dimensions of public services as discussed in the main body of this chapter are equally relevant as influences upon the organisational structure of voluntary agencies.

No categorisation of voluntary services has been attempted, except to differentiate between 'philanthropy' and 'mutal aid'. In conclusion, however, it is suggested that differences in scope and type of activity, in scale, in degree of permanence, in sources of financial support, in dependence upon voluntary workers, and in constitutional structure, both influence the forms which voluntary agencies take, and contribute to the infinite variety which may be regarded either as one of the major strengths of the voluntary sector as a whole or as a source of a variety of problems. Perhaps the most important point of difference amongst services which are called 'voluntary' however, is that they vary extensively in their degree of voluntaryness. The aim has been to illustrate two general theses. The first of these is that public as well as other influences modify the nature of voluntary social service organisations. The second is that, as in the public sector, organisational structures and processes are modified by the nature of social services of which the formal organisations (or individual agencies) through which such services are implemented, are but a part.

Politically, voluntary social services may be perceived as implementing a variety of social functions in addition to any specific services which they may provide to immediate beneficiaries; and in this respect also they are comparable with statutory ones. From one political standpoint they may be seen as 'gap fillers' whose role is properly ephemeral, and one which should diminish as and when government assumes extended responsibilities. Alternatively, one may accept Beveridge's view that 'the State cannot see to the rendering of all the services that are necessary to make a good society';[46] or agree with Mr Heath that citizens should be free to contribute their money as they will, rather than as taxpayers, to the provision of voluntary rather than statutory social services. Indeed if Mr Heath's speech serves to illustrate the existence of inter-connections between both kinds of service at the levels of both individual citizenship and of local and central government, it is perhaps more particularly interesting in its revelation of the political ideology to which it gives expression.

The overriding point which these examples of political attitudes are intended to illustrate, is that whatever the nature of any formal arrangements which may bind particular voluntary services to the institutions of government, on a broad front the place of voluntary social services in contemporary society, no less than that of statutory ones, is of political as well as practical significance. Beveridge's assertion, already quoted, that voluntary action is part of public policy, may be taken as a statement of fact, or as a statement of value, or as both. In any case, it postulates the existence of a political dimension of voluntary social services, by which the roles of those who work within them, whether as volunteers, or as salaried social workers, or as administrators, are inevitably modified. To sum up: social work roles and administrative ones, in voluntary as well as in statutory social service organisations, are best understood if the existence of public and political influences upon them is acknowledged. With the kinds of qualifications which are in any case always required in the application of generalisations to particular situations, the factors discussed in the main body of this chapter in relation to public social services are relevant to voluntary ones too.

Throughout this chapter, as in the analysis of professionalisation in chapter 1, social work itself has intentionally not been placed in the centre of the picture. In the discussion of statutory social services, it has been presented as an activity instrumental to the implementation of public policy, which itself also influences the forms taken by voluntary action. The aim has been to stress that the development and implementation of social services are characterised by public participation of a kind which initiates, supports, modifies and may even (as happened in the case of Child Care Officers) abolish the roles of those who work within them. The general thesis is that the development of social work is inextricably linked with the development of social policy, and that the administration of statutory social services is a process in which the 'public' as well as the 'professional' element must constitute a point of reference. This is an assumption which will underlie all that is said throughout the rest of the book. But if the public nature of the context in which the majority of social workers are employed now seems likely to be a permanent factor as far ahead as one can see, it is, of course, not a constant one. On the one hand, relationships between the 'public' and the 'professional' dimensions of social work could be said to be so inter-connected that the nature of social work itself cannot begin to be defined without reference to publicly expressed expectations of it. On the other hand, in the day-to-day implementation of social services the relationship may be either so rigid or so flexible, so congruous or so conflicting, so clear or so imprecise, that the form which it takes in specific and immediate circumstances as well as in more general and long-term perspectives, must be a continuous concern both of social workers themselves, and of those who manage the organisations within which social workers are employed.

Additionally, if this inter-connection of the public and the professional aspects of social work services is a matter of fact, it is also a constant source of problems of value. The existence and the development of public policy, as an influence on the nature of social work, gives rise at every level of social service administration to questions about the balance which people with very diverse standpoints believe ought to exist between public control and professional discretion.

Social work roles in public services have been suggested as being three-dimensional. So far the emphasis has been on two of these dimensions: those aspects of their roles which social workers attempt to define for themselves as members of a particular occupational group, strongly influenced by the concept of professionalism, and those which are with varying degrees of specificity assigned to them as participants in the implementation of public policy. Some may find this an unacceptable conception of the basis upon which their own roles ought to be defined. Others may consider it to be either realistic or acceptable or both. Even for those who resist it, a perception of the interaction of the professional and public determinants of the forms which social work takes, may provide a frame of reference for attempts to understand the nature of the reality with which they have to contend. There is, however, a third dimension, within which the first two must typically find expression. Social workers, who may be defined as members of a particular occupational group, and who work within social services, are also members of organisations: and it is to a consideration of the nature of organisations that we must now turn.

Chapter three

Organisations

An organisation can generally be viewed from several quite different positions, and each can yield some useful truths.

C. Perrow

It is not without significance that much of the most influential literature in the development of social work theory until the late 1960s was written by Americans whose prototype delivery system (although this is a term not then in use) was a private case-work service. It was in this context that in 1957 Greenwood made the assertion, referred to in chapter 1, that social work in the USA constituted a profession. Professionally trained social workers, as members of social work agencies and with professional supervision, provided services of a type which it was at the discretion of the agency to offer to clients whom it was likewise at the discretion of the agency to select, and who themselves sought social work help. The model which predominated as the basis of professional aspirations, both status-wise and methodologically, was a medical one, and the extensive employment of trained social workers in public social services was, until President Kennedy launched the war on poverty, largely part of an unforeseeable future. The organisations in which trained social workers were until then typically employed in the USA were dominated by the professional culture of their employees, and their primary purpose was to provide a case-work service. They were appropriately referred to and perceived as 'social work agencies' in a very literal sense of the term.

'Agency' remains a term which social workers, although probably few other people, use to refer to the units of organisation in which they are employed. In particular, it probably still dominates both the literature of social work theory and the discussion in training courses of the settings in which students do fieldwork placements. Because of its essentially professional origins and usage, the term probably carries connotations of what social workers think Probation Offices or Local

Authority Social Services Departments or whatever ought to be like, and ought to be doing. If the preceding discussion of the nature of social services has any validity, however, the use of any term which implies that the provision of a social work service on terms set by social workers is the unequivocal *raison d'être* of the systems within which social workers are typically employed in the Britain of the 1970s, it may distort rather than clarify the nature of the employment situations in which they find themselves.

It is only within the last ten years that the term 'organisation' has come into use in this context. The idea which the substance of this chapter is an attempt to justify, is that a neutral concept of 'organisation' offers a much broader base from which to attempt to understand the nature of the social worker's employment situation than does the professionally conceived idea of 'agency': although this can obviously, whenever it seems useful, be incorporated into one's concept of 'organisation'. If social workers are involved in an activity to which professional criteria are widely considered to be relevant, and if they are participants in the implementation of social policy, so also, like civil servants or coalminers or teachers, they are typically employees in organisations. Attention will be concentrated in this chapter on the organisational context within which work is done and which, in the case of social work, both affects and is affected by the professional and political factors which have already been considered.

In so far as the essence of professional activity is believed to lie in the service with which the individual practitioner provides each client, it is not surprising that a conception of the social worker's role as a member of an organisation has been peripheral to social work theory itself. Although teaching about organisations may be included in training courses, this is a very different matter from the development of a theory of social work to which the organisational dimension of social work practice is intrinsic. The model of social work presented by Pincus and Minahan,[1] which identifies the organisation as a possible target system, both provides a rationale for incorporating an organisational dimension into social work theory, and offers system theory as a starting point. A further distinction has to be made, however, between an emphasis on the role of the social worker *vis-à-vis* an organisation on the one hand, and on the nature of organisations on the other. Pincus and Minahan emphasise the former. Here the emphasis is on the latter, the hypothesis being that the very nature of social work itself is affected by the organisational statuses of social workers. This is by no means to deny the usefulness of the idea of the organisation as a 'target system', but rather to emphasise the notion that target systems need to be understood as well as to be aimed at. If this is indeed the case, an understanding of the nature of organisations is as relevant to those whose work is directly with clients as it is to those whose positions are essentially administrative or organisational.

Systematic thinking about the nature of organisations originated with the 'scientific managers', followed by social psychologists such as Elton Mayo and his associates in what has come to be called the 'human relations' school.[2] The predominant concern of both approaches was to expound a rational basis for the development of more effective methods of management, and each can be said to have been biased in considering organisations primarily from a management point of view. Thus if as has been suggested, the concept of 'social work agency' is value-loaded, in so far as social workers imbue it with their ideas about what their own organisations ought to be doing, so, it might be argued, the concept of 'organisation' is equally open to prejudiced use by those whose primary interest is in efficient management. An attempt will be made in this chapter to present an analysis of the concept of 'organisation' which is comparable in its neutrality to the discussion of professionalisation in chapter 1. The aim will be to construct a systematic picture of ways in which social scientists have looked at organisations, and to illustrate some of their conclusions about what organisations are like. This is clearly a very different matter from saying what they ought to be like: but it will later be argued (in chapters 4 and 5) that those who work in organisations, or who carry responsibility for what is done within them, both can and should attempt to modify them, in relation to the purposes which they believe those organisations ought to be serving. In the case of organisations as of professionalisation, a clearer understanding of the nature of the phenomenon in question is relevant to practical decision-making by individuals, both about what can be done and about what ought to be done, in their own particular situations.

This is not to say that social scientists either do provide totally objective and comprehensive representations of 'real life' organisations or are ever likely to be able to do so. No one organisation is exactly like any other; organisation theorists are influenced in their perceptions by the particular purposes for which they are studying organisations; and in any case, like other social scientists, they are inevitably selective in the factors which they take into account as they pursue the unattainable goal of seeing organisations 'whole'. What they can do, however, is to attempt to identify characteristics which all organisations share, as well as those which differentiate some types of organisation from others. They can provide ways of looking at organisations, and at the problems which arise within them, which have been developed out of systematic and dispassionate analysis, rather than idiosyncratically out of personal experience. Moreover, and perhaps most usefully of all, they can develop a language which enables both themselves and those who work in organisations to communicate more effectively amongst each other about the problems and tasks which confront them.

As Olive Stevenson has said in relation to knowledge for social work, the social sciences are changing fast, and we are on shifting sands.[3] Even the frames of reference which can put some order into our ways of looking at and interpreting social situations, are both subjective and selective. They may be related to particular political ideologies, they may overlap and conflict with each other, and they may be based on concepts in the social sciences which are subsequently found wanting. It seems unrealistic to believe that we are in a situation in which we shall move over time ever nearer to a complete picture of reality. Rather, as was suggested in the preface, the history of social science seems likely to be formed of the emergence of new paradigms: one paradigm replaces another which has been recognised as inadequate to explain the nature of the particular aspect of reality under consideration. We do well, therefore, to be cautious, if not sceptical, in our attitudes to any attempt by social scientists to explain what organisations are like. On the other hand, we all as individuals construct our own ways of looking at the situations in which we find ourselves: and there may be something to be said for doing this in ways which incorporate knowledge derived from sources external to our personal, and therefore limited and random, experience. It is with these reservations and justifications in mind that the following illustrative discussion of organisation theory is to be read.

The social sciences are founded on the belief that there are regularities in social life which may be identified, and the causes of which may be amenable to explanation. Two social sciences in particular, namely sociology and social psychology, have predominated in the examination of regularities in organisations. Although however, social psychologists and sociologists share organisations as a field of study, there are fundamental and distinguishable differences in their ways of looking at them. Very briefly, the sociologist may be said to be interested in clarifying the nature of organisations as systems of interlocking roles or patterned behaviour, which are themselves interconnected with other social systems or institutions, such as for example political systems or the market. On the whole, sociologists are interested in systems rather than in individuals or personalities. Organisational psychologists, on the other hand, tend to perceive organisations as groupings of people. On the whole, they are interested in the ways in which individuals or small groups behave and relate to each other in organisations. As each approach is centred on the same phenomenon, that is to say on organisations, clearly each will be of limited value if the other is ignored, either by social scientists themselves, or by those for whom day-to-day reality is all of a piece and who wish to make practical use of what theory has to offer, without worrying about nice distinctions between academic disciplines.

For social workers whose skills and whose professional interests are with people, whether as individuals or in small groups, it may be that the approach of the social psychologist is both more congenial, and more likely to be convincing than that of the sociologist. Most people, social workers or not, probably find it easier to think of organisations as composed of individuals either getting on well together or being awkward, than as systems of which some of the most influential characteristics have little to do with the personalities of those who are employed within them. On the other hand, sociology is now of widely accepted relevance in education for the practice of social work itself, both for the light which it can throw on the nature of the society in which both social workers and clients find themselves and, as Heraud has maintained, for its 'relevance to the understanding of the individual act'.[4] Furthermore, as social stratification or social deviance or the institution of the family may be studied, and in some important senses understood, without reference to specific individuals, so it may be argued can organisations.

What follows is intended both to illustrate this suggestion and, more specifically, to suggest the relevance of organisation theory to the clarification of the nature of the reality within which the roles of social workers are defined. Even more than if this were a textbook on organisation theory itself, it has been difficult to decide what to put in and what to leave out. The two criteria which have affected the conscious selection process have been the importance of particular concepts or perspectives within organisation theory itself, and their potential usefulness to social workers who wish to develop their own systematic frames of reference.

Bureaucracy

The term 'bureaucracy' is commonly used disparagingly. Here it is presented for consideration as representing a neutral concept, and in particular as a paradigm which offers a framework for identifying and subsequently discussing some aspects of the nature of organisations. Analyses of the concept as developed by Weber are so readily available elsewhere[5] as not to call for reiteration here. Silverman, however, provides a very concise and convenient summary of Weber's characterisation of the ideal-type bureaucracy, as 'a clearly defined hierarchy where office holders have very specific functions and apply universalistic rules in a spirit of formalistic impersonality'.[6] With that definition in mind, it is possible to consider first the potentialities and limitations of the concept itself as an analytical tool, and second some of the prescriptions for action which normative interpretations of the ideal type model may embody.

To begin with, it should be emphasised that everything said in chapter 1 about ideal-type models in relationship to professions applies also to bureaucracy. Thus although the concept represents an attempt to incorporate the features by which formal organisations are typified, it is not to be concluded that all formal organisations display all these characteristics to the same degree. Nor can it be said that all the attributes of such organisations are incorporated into this one abstract model. As an ideal-type model of a profession provides us with only one out of a variety of frames of reference for analysing the nature of 'professional' occupations, so an ideal type model of a 'bureaucracy' constitutes only one basis for the consideration of the nature of organisations. It can be used to throw light particularly on the nature of authority relationships and on the division of labour within organisations: but at least in its early form, it emphasises only the formal and impersonal aspects of organisational relationships, and it attributes a static quality to organisational structures. In the history of organisation theory, Weber's ideal type model of a bureaucracy has perhaps been most important as a paradigm: as a representation of reality in a new form, which has been a fruitful source of thinking directed towards the identification of attributes of organisations which the bureaucratic model itself does not incorporate.

Bureaucracy was presented by Weber, in what Silverman describes as 'an uncharacteristic moment of dogmatism,'[7] as the most 'efficient' type of organisation. Later social scientists have joined with laymen in querying this, and have attempted to identify the functions which bureaucratic forms of organisation serve, and those which they do not. According to the purposes which one thinks an organisation ought to be serving, it is possible to use such functional analyses as a basis upon which to decide whether, and for what purposes, and in what ways, organisations ought to be more, or less, bureaucratically structured and administered.

The functions of bureaucratic forms of organisation have been variously defined,[8] but have been taken to include stability and permanence, role security, the rational deployment of individual skills, and impartiality of treatment for both members of the organisation and outsiders in contact with it. Dysfunctions in relation to efficiency have been taken to include ritualism and overconformity, inflexibility and resistance to change, restrictions on the imaginative use of individual skills and initiative, and the routinisation of procedures for handling situations which ideally require individual treatment. It is easy to see that such classifications of bureaucratic functions and dysfunctions cannot be purely objective, but must be related to a concept of desired purposes. Thus, for example, the protection from the public which a bureaucracy affords to its members may be functional to the security of the organisation itself as a smoothly running machine, but dysfunctional to the welfare of individual citizens.

The concept of bureaucracy may be used to clarify what particular organisations are actually like. It may also provide a basis from which one can consider how they ought to be structured and administered in relation to the ends which it is thought they should serve. In this second respect, before crying 'down with bureaucracy', social workers might consider points such as the following. First, in circumstances in which the just treatment of clients requires impartiality in the allocation of goods or services, criteria of eligibility must be formally established and impartially implemented, and not be left to the discretion of individuals. Those who argue for the restriction of discretionary social security benefits are in fact advocating an extension of the bureaucratic element in the administration of Supplementary Benefits. Second, both formal authority structures and written rules and regulations can afford support and protection to individual members of an organisation; and indeed may be said to constitute responsibility-sharing devices. Third, there may be certain activities within even a professional organisation which can be most easily and efficiently carried out if routinised on a bureaucratic basis. The practical problem may thus be not to decide for or against 'bureaucracy' once and for all, but rather to discriminate between the purposes which bureaucratic methods of organisation can serve, and those which they cannot, and to attempt to act accordingly.

Of all the concepts evolved throughout the history of organisation theory, bureaucracy has probably been the most powerful influence on the ways in which people at large think of organisations: and yet to attempt to summarise even the most formal organisation exclusively in terms of the characteristics identified in the definition quoted above is, as the rest of this chapter will constitute an attempt to demonstrate, to take too limited a view. It is suggested, however, that the attributes of organisations now to be discussed do not so much replace the concept of bureaucracy, as constitute supplements to it.

Organisations as processes

The pure bureaucracy, were it ever to exist, would be an essentially static organisation, with permanence the major characteristic of its structure, and of the activities of its members. Peter Blau's classic study of two bureaucratic organisations, however, revealed that ceaseless change was characteristic of each of them. The 'dynamics of bureaucracy' was the expressive term he used to refer to movements within formal organisations, of a kind which the ideal type model of bureaucracy does not incorporate.[9] The nature of life itself, as summed up in Blau's quotation from Heraclitus to the effect that 'one cannot step twice into the same river', would alone seem to offer ample support for the view that whatever resistance there may be to it, and whatever built-in protection there may be against it, change must be a feature of any system in which work involves interaction between people, and in which there are exchanges between that system and an external environment which is itself in continuous process of change.

This notion of organisations (like professions) as processes, implies that they are to be perceived as changing even as we look at them: what a Social Services Department was like yesterday it is no longer like today, for behaviour and events, both within it and outside it, have already made it something different. It is always 'in process of becoming', and never arrives at a final equilibrium, either internally or in relation to the outside world. But the concept of organisations as processes does not preclude an analytical approach that also makes use of the concept of bureaucracy. For example, these two aspects of the reality of organisations may be used together as a starting point for considering some of the major problem areas of organisational life, such as the relationship, whether actual or desirable, between stability and change, or between formality and informality. In so far, however, as the concept of process offers an accurate reflection of what organisations are like, it means that those who work in organisations are part of a dynamic situation in which it is unrealistic to assume that a final point of stability can ever be reached.

The nature and implications of change in organisations, late though they were to be incorporated into organisational theory, now constitute one of its central themes.[10] There is space here to refer to only one point, which indeed relates not only to change but to other aspects of organisations. Theorists make a distinction which, while it may sometimes be difficult for those directly experiencing the impact of complex organisational situations to make, may nevertheless be of real practical importance. This is the distinction between changes in individuals and changes in *organisational* variables. Individuals may change, for example, during secondment for training, and then return to organisations in which no arrangements have been made to accommodate their newly acquired knowledge and skills. At the same time, many people will have experienced situations in which it has been structural change, such as a reallocation of duties within a particular unit of organisation, or the establishment of new sub-units such as area offices, which has most significantly affected what they as individuals are able to do. Thus the notion of organisational change, while it incorporates that of individual or personal change, also embodies the idea that the process of change is intrinsic to organisations as systems which embody features which are in essence impersonal.

Organisations as systems

As has been implied in the identification of organisations as processes, the development of organisation theory has seen a shift from concentration on distinct aspects of organisation (such as those incorporated into the bureaucratic model) to a broader outlook which has concentrated on the interrelatedness of different components of organisational life, including those which the bureaucratic model embodies. Such an outlook finds expression not only in the idea of formal organisations as processes of planned or unplanned change, but in the development of frames of reference in which they are perceived as systems which both incorporate internal sub-systems, and interact with systems external to themselves. The bureaucratic model infers a homogeneous structure within which salaried employees perform clearly defined tasks, and in which authority is hierarchically distributed through lines headed by a chief executive. The boundaries of a bureaucracy are by definition closed, for a bureaucracy incorporates the behaviour only of paid employees. Some system theorists also have chosen to ignore extra-organisational factors, and have considered it useful to study organisations as 'closed' systems the nature of which is, by implication, determined internally. Others have considered that the lines bounding organisations can be easily drawn and, while acknowledging the potential significance of external variables, have not considered them integral to the analysis of organisations themselves.

A third approach, selected for consideration here, is that in which organisations are perceived as 'open' systems which are not self-contained, but inter-connected, if to varying degrees and in varying ways, with systems external to themselves. An open system approach implies neither internal homogeneity, nor set organisational boundaries. On the first count, a Social Services Department, or a Probation Office, or a medical social work unit, would be perceived as internally composed of an interrelated series of processes and a complexity of inter-connected parts, which can be distinguished from each other only with varying degrees of objectivity. It would be interrelationships and processes, rather than one or other analytically separable aspect of the organisation, which would be the focus of study. On the second count, an open system approach would view any such 'agency' as a system inaccessible to understanding unless perceived as itself acting upon, and acted upon by, systems external to itself such as, for example, the Social Services Committee of the Local Authority and other manifestations of the institution of local government; or the judicial system; or the nursing and medical hierarchies of the hospital. Such an approach may be particularly useful in illuminating the role of the head of a social service or social work organisation, whose work may be as much with systems external to his 'own department' as within it. Moreover,

71

the external systems which so impinge upon the operation of a particular organisation are not perceived simply as extensions of that organisation, but also as components of other systems by which they themselves are influenced as, for example, a Social Services Committee is part of the political, as distinct from the administrative, system of local government.

Thus internally, an organisation is seen as a network of interacting, overlapping, conflicting or co-operating sub-systems or interdependent parts, each part receiving something from others, influenced by the behaviour of others, and itself behaving in ways which have consequences both for other sub-systems and for the organisation as a whole. On the other hand, from a societal point of view, the organisation itself is a sub-system of other and larger systems, and its integration or conflict with these systems directly affects both what it does and how it does it. An open system approach to an understanding of the workings of a Social Services Department would consider, together, the department itself as the system, its internal units, structures and processes as sub-systems, and the political and administrative institutions of central and local government as super-systems which both provide it with work and set limits to its autonomy.

Such an approach can be useful if it helps to systematise one's comprehension both of the inter-connectedness of organisational parts, and of the range of external influences to which particular organisations are exposed, and in relation to which they have to function.

An open system approach may also serve to focus attention on the nature and significance of an organisation's boundaries and environment. Organisations are seen as dependent upon exchanges at their boundaries with an environment which sanctions their existence, influences the nature of the work they do, and provides them with resources. They may indeed be perceived as systems of exchange, which take in resources, receive instructions of varying degrees of explicitness, and transform the resources into goods or services which constitute their output.

The concept of organisational boundaries is interesting if only because any attempt to define the boundaries of an organisation is likely to reveal how difficult it is in practice to do so. Katz and Kahn suggest that boundaries are demarcation lines, both physical and psychological, which both constitute barriers to interaction between people on the 'inside' and those on the 'outside', and also facilitate it.[11] The physical boundary constituted by a top security prison building is easily enough distinguished; but if the impact of the Home Office on the ways in which prisons are run is taken into account, it is much more difficult to set a meaningful boundary to the prison as an organisation. Similarly it would appear to be unrealistic to limit one's conception of any social service or social work organisation to what goes on within a particular building, or even to the activities of salaried employees. Interaction between those employees and, for example, volunteers, foster mothers, clients and committee members or significant members of the public, blurs the tidy boundary line implicit in the ideal type mode of bureaucracy. If organisations are distinct from their social environment (in so far as it makes any sense to refer to a university, or a prison, or a Social Services Department, or a coal mine as an organisation), so also they differ both from each other and individually over time, in the nature of the distinctions that can be made. They are to varying degrees permeable from outside. Perceptions of organisations both as processes and as open systems interacting with an external environment, connote the boundaries of organisations as continuously shifting, and as determined not only internally, but by behaviour within significant systems in the outside world.

Formal and informal elements

All organisations in which people are employed can be described as 'formal', when it seems necessary to stress a distinction from other forms of social grouping, such as friendship groups or families which, as both processes and systems, are less consciously planned and less deliberately structured, and whose membership is much less routinely changed:[12] which are, to put it simply, less 'organised'. Even if, however, as in this book, the term organisation is used as a synonym for 'formal organisation' in the above sense, it is easily apparent that informality pervades organisational life.

The bureaucratic ideal type model of organisations has already been referred to as limited in that it does not incorporate the phenomenon of movement, process, change or environment. Nor does it acknowledge the relevance of behaviour outside a network of standardised roles. Beyond the confines of a bureaucratic frame of reference, organisation theorists have recognised that organisations consist of both formal and informal elements, and have turned their attention to exploring the nature of relationships between these, and their significance for organisational performance. This approach is characterised by Blau and Scott in their comparative study of formal organisations: 'It is impossible to understand the nature of a formal organisation without investigating the network of informal relations and the unofficial norms, as well as the formal hierarchy of authority and the official bodies of rules, since the formally instituted and the informally emerging patterns are inextricably intertwined'.[13] More specifically, Blau and Scott consider that no official charts, plans, blueprints or manuals can ever provide for every situation with which members of an organisation may be confronted, or completely determine their behaviour. They suggest indeed that informal behaviour is nurtured by the very formality of such devices. Official rules cannot be sufficiently specific to cover all situations, and informal practices have to be resorted to for solutions. Unofficial and socially determined norms are apt to develop, as regulators of the ways in which individual members of organisations behave. Complex networks of social relations and of statuses evolve within groups and between them, on the basis of personal abilities and affinities and hostilities, and as distinct from officially assigned roles. Such factors may contribute to the emergence of situations in which formally defined groupings, formally prescribed procedures, and formally constituted authority structures, may be accompanied by the existence of informal ones which individuals or small groups within an organisation, for reasons of their own, have found it either organisationally useful or personally congenial to develop. Selznick approaches the topic of informal aspects of formal organisations by suggesting that the formal design can never fully reflect the nature of an organisation, 'for the obvious reason that no abstract plan or pattern can ... exhaustively describe an empirical reality'.[14] The formal structure of an organisation, according to Selznick, is only one aspect of a social structure made up of individuals who act as total persons, and not simply in terms of roles to which they have been formally assigned.

Thus organisation theorists acknowledge the co-existence of formal and informal elements as part of the reality of organisations: as surely must anyone who has thought about the nature of any organisation in which he has been employed. Of greater interest is the nature and significance of this co-existence in particular organisations. Moreover, in this respect also, organisations are dynamic. As the terms 'bureaucratisation' and 'debureaucratisation' imply, they may become, or be made either more or less formal than they were. An understanding of the nature of this process, and of the implications of particular changes, is of relevance to members of organisations (whether industrial workers, or managers, or social work practitioners or administrators) who inevitably participate in both systems, but who may also wish to modify them.

A perception of organisations as embodying both formal and informal systems, which both change and can be changed in relationship to each other, may both illuminate the existing state of particular organisations, and help to focus attention on problems inherent in the management of organisational development. There is ample evidence[15] that informal systems within an organisation may either facilitate the performance of its formal mission, or seriously impede it. Informal systems may supplement the formal ones and be congruous with them; or they may constitute a form of resistance to them, and conflict with them. They arise out of 'personal' rather than 'official' responses to situations, and they may serve either personal or organisational purposes, or conceivably both. The co-existence of the two types of system is a fact of organisational life; and the nature of particular patterns of co-existence, and the management of their development, is not only a matter of concern for managers, but of potential significance for all individuals whose work is in an organisational setting.

People in organisations

Something of what has been already said implies that organisation theory suggests that organisations are not to be understood simply as groupings of people, if only because they are also constituted of more or less formally structured sets of positions and duties, which may persist irrespective of the membership of any particular organisation at any one time. True though it be that only people and not organisations can act, and that what we call 'organisational' behaviour always has its origins in the actions of people, organisations also acquire or inherit the products of such behaviour (in the form of, for example, written rules and regulations, or organisations charts which set out particular formal structures), which exert their own impersonal influences long after their human originators have disappeared from the scene. In some instances, as with statutory rules and regulations, the original formulators are neither personally identifiable, nor in any direct way participants in the implementation of such rules. Perrow sums up such aspects of organisations as the enduring patterns of behaviour that give an organisation its form and structure.[16] What Perrow is in fact emphasising is the pattern, rather than behaviour as a function of individual actors. For reasons such as these, it is meaningful to consider people as components of or participants in organisational systems, rather than as constituting the totality of any organisation.

There appears to be no end to the literature on people in organisations, and much of it, if only because of the equivocal nature of man himself, gives rise to more questions than it answers. In general, however, the picture which emerges is the two-dimensional one of people whose co-operative participation organisational effectiveness requires, but with needs of their own with the meeting of which organisational requirements may conflict. Two major perspectives on people in organisations are also to be identified: that of the psychologist who focuses directly on people as individuals or in small groups, and that of the sociologists whose interest is in the nature of the structures and systems within which people act.

Silverman provides a succinct exposition of the approach typical of organisational psychology as follows. Individuals are motivated by needs which directly influence their behaviour and may serve to explain it. There is a basic conflict between the needs of individuals and the goals of organisations, which is best met by changing the organisational structure in order to minimise such conflict. This can be done by encouraging worker participation in decision-making, by the formation of stable work groups, by good communication and expressive supervision, and by a shift away from bureaucratic hierarchies of authority.[17]

What has perhaps been most interesting about the development of organisational psychology has been the combination of postulations about the nature of man and about his needs on the one hand, and prescriptions for the management of organisations on the other. The 'old school' of scientific management assumed that man in (industrial) organisations was a creature whose behaviour was essentially economically motivated, but who also tended to be lazy: management should both stimulate his economic motivation and closely supervise and control his behaviour. Subsequently the human relations school, while denying a conflict of interest between industrial worker and employer, postulated a need for membership of satisfying work-groups within the organisation: efficient management would respect this need, and by making workers happier would make them more productive. More recently, psychologists have made suppositions about human needs without implying that man's organisational experience and behaviour can be separated off from the rest of his life. For example, Maslow's hierarchy of human needs, which training for social work may have made familiar to social workers, culminates in the need for self-actualisation whatever the sphere of activity in which an individual may be engaged. Organisationally, a concept of man as 'self-actualising' implies a type of management which will enable people to pursue their own self-fulfilment: and thus McGregor concludes that 'the essential task of management is to arrange organisational conditions and methods of operation so that people can achieve their own goals best by directing their own efforts towards organisational objectives'.[18]

If, however, Maslow's concept of self-actualising man can serve as an example of the psychological approach to the topic of people in organisations, it also embodies some of the problematic aspects of such an approach. Can such a concept of man be said to be scientifically validated, or does it rest primarily on the personal social philosophy and value system of the psychologist? Can it be said to explain or predict human behaviour, or does it rather imply both a view of how human beings should perceive each other, and a prescription for how they should behave towards each other? Can it be said to be of universal application, or may it apply to some people and to some situations more than to others? As for McGregor's prescription, it seems inadequately to cover either the possibility of irreducible conflicts between organisational and personal objectives, or situations in which the self-actualisation of one person may mean that the aspirations of another are thwarted.

Etzioni on the other hand faces this dilemma head on: 'a point is reached in every organisation where happiness and efficiency cease to support each other. Not all work can be well paid or gratifying, and not all regulations and orders can be made acceptable'.[19] He goes on to suggest a more modest objective than that espoused by the 'self-actualisation' psychologists, when he suggests that 'the problem of the modern organisation is thus how to construct human groupings that are as rational as possible, and at the same time produce a minimum of side effects and a maximum of satisfaction'.[20]

Perrow likewise, while acknowledging that sociologists adopt a cruder concept of human nature than do psychologists, is sceptical of an approach which relies on an understanding of individual psychology, rather than of structural problems, to explain or modify organisational behaviour. He provides a counterbalance to Selznick when he suggests that people in organisations react to each other not simply as individuals, but as occupiers of particular roles. Perrow's emphasis is placed on the roles which people occupy, rather than on the nature of their personalities,[21] and his prescription for management is as follows: 'it has been my experience that manipulating the structure, arranging the goals, and grasping the nature of the environment, are more practical and efficient ways of dealing with organisational problems, than trying to change human behaviour directly'.[22] An illustration of a practical application of such an approach may be taken from a university setting, as follows. The personality of professors is a major derterminant of the ways in which departments are run. At the same time, the formal structure of universities places great power in the hands of professors. Supposing that it were desired to minimise the effect of the personalities of professors upon departments, a more effective approach than trying to change these personalities might be to modify the existing power structure in such a way as to lessen professorial autonomy.

It is perhaps on this matter of people in organisations that the potentially complementary approaches of sociological and of psychological organisation theory can be most clearly distinguished from each other. At one end of a continuum, organisations may be perceived as consisting of individual personalities interacting with each other, for their own as well as for organisational purposes. At the other end, they may be conceptualised in ideal-type models such as, for example, the bureaucratic model, in which the emphasis is upon the nature of the structures and systems within which actors implement roles. Although it may be easiest for members of organisations to think of them as being composed essentially of individual personalities, the current state of organisation theory seems to indicate that they will be nearer the mark if they also seek to understand the structural causes of the situations in which they find themselves.

Technologies, people and environment

Organisations have already been referred to as systems which receive instructions and resources from outside, and convert resources into the goods or services which constitute their output. This conversion involves the use of knowledge and skills to do with tools and machinery, or of professional knowledge and expertise in the provision of services as distinct from goods. Those who emphasise the importance of 'technologies' in the life of organisations describe organisations as socio-technical systems, located within an influential environment, of which the central problems have to do with 'the technical requirements of the task and the human needs of those performing it'.[23]

The organisational significance of technologies in the production process (which is here taken to include the production of services as well as goods) was first identified by Joan Woodward, whose empirical research revealed that firms using similar technologies had similar organisational structures. For example, the proportion of managers and supervisors to others tended to be highest where the work was technically complex; and organisations in which the need for technical innovation was great tended to be less bureaucratised than those in which the appropriate production methods were routine. Perhaps the most important hypothesis for which Woodward and others have produced so much empirical evidence that it cannot be safely ignored, is that technology is a determinant of organisational structure. In so far as this is the case, it means that those who manage organisations are not free either to structure them or to run them on the basis of the simple assumption that 'organisations are people': the nature of the work to be done itself tends to impose an organisational form of its own.

If the influence of technology on organisational structure may help to explain the forms which that structure takes, a socio-technical approach may also help to illuminate certain organisational problems such as the following. First, the particular technology which the work to be done involves may be the source of structures and processes which conflict with the needs of an organisation's members. The automated car industry might provide illustrations of this. Second, complex organisations are composed of sub-systems, the work of which may require the use of a variety of technologies, each demanding and tending to procure its own particular form of organisational structure. The nature of the work to be done may affect the degree of bureaucratisation not only of different organisations, but of particular sub-systems of the same organisation, where members may be required to co-operate with each other in spite of widely varying authority structures. Third, technological innovation may radically affect the functioning of existing social systems within an organisation; as the processes of mechanisation and automation in industry demonstrate.

The work which an organisation has to do in order to survive has been described as its primary task.[24] A single primary task may, however, be impossible to isolate, as in the case of teaching hospitals which both treat patients and teach medical students. Furthermore, an organisation's primary task may be differently defined by different people, according to what they think it ought to be. The most realistic definition in any particular case may demand an assessment of what an organisation actually does, rather than a reliance upon what people say it does.

A very brief reference to Local Authority Social Services Departments may serve to illustrate some of the complexities which the notion of organisations as socio-technical systems with primary tasks to perform may be used to reveal.

What is the primary task of such a department? Is it to provide a social work service to clients on the basis of need as defined by social workers? Is it to implement certain duties of the Local Authority as laid down in legislation? Supposing it is to do both, what kind of organisational structure does each task tend to produce; and each task need? It could be said that Social Services Departments have work to do which ranges along a continuum from that of which the content may be largely defined by social workers, such as case-work support for the mother of a subnormal child, to that which is very closely set about with statutory rules and regulations, as in the implementation of Care and Control Orders. The kind of organisational structure which the social work at one end of the continuum might tend to produce if this were the only kind of work the department had to do, might be significantly different from that which work at the other end tends to give rise to. An additional problem may be that the technology (or expertise) which staff of the department consider to be appropriate to the work to be done, is either imperfectly understood, or possibly thought to be inappropriate, in those parts of the organisation's environment (or super-systems) which make demands upon it.

The socio-technical approach would suggest that the forms which the structure of a Social Services Department takes are influenced by the complexity of the work which it has to do, and by the demands made upon it by the environment, including the super-system of local government, in relation to which it has to operate. It also, however, acknowledges the existence of needs amongst those who do an organisation's work; and in organisations employing social workers, these may include the need to participate in defining both the primary task and the nature of the expertise which its performance requires.

To sum up, this particular approach suggests that there are three major determinants of the forms which organisational structures take: the technologies intrinsic to the work the organisation has to do, the demands made upon the organisation by its environment, and the demands of its members. However, it is one thing to suggest that these three factors themselves determine organisational structure; another to say they require rather than determine particular structures; another to say only that they are factors to be taken into account when organisational change is being planned; and yet another to suggest that the promotion of compatibilities between them ought to be the concern of managers seeking to enhance organisational stability and efficiency. Indeed, as is the case with other interpretations of the nature of organisations, the analytical elements in the socio-technical approach are not always easily distinguished from the prescriptive ones. One prescription is at least implied if not made explicit: if different technologies, different environments and different participants produce, or require, different types of organisational structure, then there is no one most efficient form of organisation. That will be the most efficient which is both right for a particular technology and also minimises conflict with the demands made both by the environment and by the organisation's members. These, however, may vary from sub-system to sub-system, and are not to be taken as uniform throughout the organisation as a whole.

Organisational goals

Etzioni has suggested that 'organisations are social units which pursue specific goals'.[25] Having offered this snappy definition, however, he then proceeds to an analysis of the nature of organisational goals which incidentally illustrates that one of the practical uses of organisational theory is that it can help to make explicit the ways in which things are not always as simple as they may at first seem. Reference to the equivocal nature of an organisation's primary task has already hinted that the idea that organisations have definite goals will not stand up to close examination; and three points raised by Perrow[26] seem to clinch the matter. First, it can be argued that only individuals and not organisations can have goals. Second, in trying to identify and measure goals, we may have to decide whether to consider the behaviour of all the members of an organisation, or only that of the powerful and influential ones. Third, there is the problem of distinguishing between a goal and a means: for what one person calls a goal might be seen by someone else only the means to a higher or more general end. In the face of such points as these, the assumption that an organisation has a goal upon the nature of which all its members agree and which they all combine to pursue, congenial though such an idea may be, appears to be quite unrealistic.

If the other aspects of the nature of organisations which have been presented so far in this chapter are used to consider the notion of organisational goals, additional complexities emerge into the daylight. There is the ubiquitous problem of distinguishing between 'is' and 'ought': can one distinguish between what the goals of an organisation actually are, and what they 'ought' to be? Is it safe to assume that all the participants in any particular organisation would agree on either of these points? Or that the behaviour of all of them conforms with the pursuit of goals upon which all have been agreed? May different goals be developed within different sub-systems of an organisation, or within the super-system by which it is affected? How do goals which may be pursued by informal groups relate to any officially defined goals? And how do any goals which individuals seek to pursue for themselves within an organisation correspond to official ones? If organisations are indeed processes, as well as systems, how are goals formulated, and how do they change? How appropriate are the formal structures of any particular organisation, and the technologies being used, to any goals which it is consciously intended that the organisation shall foster? How clear are the members of any organisation about the nature of its primary task, and what consensus is there about it? Are the various goals which participating individuals or sub-groups attribute to an organisation compatible with each other? May the maintenance and functioning of an organisation itself become, for at least some of its participants, an end which assumes greater immediacy than the purposes which others believe the organisation should be serving?

What organisation theory has to say about the nature of organisational goals is iconoclastic, in that it suggests that the idea of organisations having goals which can be objectively defined is unrealistic, and that any valid categorical statements about the nature of the goals of any organisation are likely to be of so general a kind as to tell us very little. To say, for example, that the goal of an industrial undertaking is to make a profit, or that of a Scottish Social Work Department to promote social welfare,[27] is to say very little indeed about what such organisational systems are really like, or about what they actually do. And yet, when such general statements are once questioned, an uncloseable Pandora's box of subsidiary, and possibly unanswerable, questions is opened. Such questions may, however, throw more light on the nature of organisations and on problems of working within them, than the assumption that organisations have goals which are definable, compatible with each other, and agreed upon by all participants can ever do.

Typologies of organisations

Reference to the bibliography at the end of this book will quickly reveal that much of the material listed as being potentially useful to social workers is neither about social work as an occupation, nor ostensibly about the kinds of organisation within which social workers are employed. Why then is it included?

There is a sense in which every human situation and experience is unique, and in which no one can ever really communicate anything to anyone else. In the last resort, no exposition of either an organisational problem or of a possible solution to it will ever completely fit the individual case. On the other hand, no intellectual or social interaction would be possible without the presumptions both that it is worthwhile to attempt to communicate across the barriers of individual experience, and that there are levels of conceptualisation at which it becomes possible to make meaningful generalisations about phenomena which are also, paradoxically, acknowledged to be unique. So in the case of organisations, attributes may be identified which all organisations share. For example, the concept of a central problem area to do with inter-connections between technologies, the nature of the work to be done, the human needs of participants, and the impact of the environment may be applicable to factories, hospitals, mines, social service organisations, universities and departments of the civil service alike. Alvin Gouldner makes the point that the value of abstract concepts derives from their usefulness for the analysis of many organisations. Specifically, he illustrates the fruitfulness of the concept of bureaucracy, traditionally associated with civil service settings, for understanding management practices and problems in a factory. Through his study of a factory, Gouldner offers insights into the nature of bureaucracy in action, which may throw light on the nature of organisations which both appear to be, and in some ways are, fundamentally different from the particular organisation which he himself selected for analysis.[28]

While some perspectives on organisations embody ideas of potentially universal relevance, and whilst it is conceded that each and every organisation is also unique, there remains a middle ground in which organisation theorists have attempted to classify organisations on the basis of characteristics which may apply to some but not to others. For example, although the concept of bureaucracy may be applicable to the analysis of any organisation, some organisations may be found to be essentially bureaucratised, and others not. The range of variables upon which attempts to categorise organisations have been based is so large as to have produced attempts to categorise the typologies themselves.[29] The primary interest of social workers, however, will be not in the construction or classification of typologies, but in their potential usefulness. According to Perrow,[30] what is needed by those who are going to work in an organisation, is some way of knowing what makes it distinctive: of conceptualising the differences between that particular organisation and another which may, or may not, be in the same line of business. Are there ways, more subtle than the obvious point that social workers are employed in them, in which organisations of which the provision of social work services is a primary task, differ from other organisations? Are there systematically identifiable ways in which Local Authority Social Services Departments, for example, differ from each other? It may be that organisations which we tend to think of as alike because they have the same title, or the same manifest functions, can differ more from each other than from organisations with which at first sight they appear to have little in common. Thus the construction of typologies constitutes an attempt to search below surface similarities for fundamental differences which some organisations share with each other.

The following examples of typologies are selected because although in none of them is social work identified as a distinguishing feature, the dissection of each may reveal something about the organisations within which social workers are employed, which a concentration on social work as their common denominator might only serve to disguise: for to say that Family Service Units, Probation Services, or Local Authority Social Services Departments are alike in that social work is the primary professional activity in all of them may tell us much less about them as organisations than may be discernible from the identification of certain differences between them.

Blau and Scott have suggested that organisations may be typed on the basis of those whose good they primarily serve: mutual benefit organisations of which the prime beneficiaries are the members, business concerns which benefit their owners, common-weal organisations which benefit the public at large, and service organisations benefitting a client group.[31] Etzioni offers a typology based on predominant types of control and of compliance with it. Organisations may be typed as coercive where control is exercised predominantly by force; utilitarian where control depends predominantly upon the remuneration offered to those who comply with it; and normative, where control is based upon appeals to personal or professional values.[32] From Etzioni comes also the typing of organisations (as distinct from occupations) as professional, semi-professional or non-professional.[33] Burns and Stalker differentiate between organisations in which technical activities are routinised and of which the environmental conditions are stable, and those which are facing complex new tasks and conditions. This is an essentially dynamic basis of categorisation, which implies that a particular organisation may change in type over time, as crucial circumstances change.[34] Goffman presents the category of 'total institution', to distinguish organisations in which there is a high degree of internal control over inmates' behaviour.[35] Yet another typology is based on the location of power, as in the concept of 'front line' organisation, where the real power to influence operational policy lies with individuals or groups at the bottom, or on the periphery, of the formal structure.[36]

These brief references suggest only the bare skeletons of a very few typologies. In conclusion, two general points may be made about these particular examples, and about organisational typologies in general. The first point is to do primarily with understanding organisations, and the second with action within them.

First, if typologies are intended to identify the distinctive features of categories of organisations, they also draw attention to ways in which particular characteristics may be shared by organisations which are superficially unalike. It is possible that more may be learned about the nature, including the problems, of a social service organisation in a period of rapid change and instability by reference to studies of factories in similar circumstances, than by assuming that because a social service organisation is different from a factory, no extrapolations from studies of industry can be made. Second, most typologies incorporate ideas about the kinds of management which particular types of organisation may tend to produce or be said to require. Thus Blau and Scott suggest that each of their types of organisation has its special managerial problems,[37] and Burns and Stalker associate the appropriateness of two quite distinct management methods with their two main organisational types. Dorothy Smith considers that 'front line' organisations present distinctive problems of control, which call for appropriate supervisory structures.[38]

To sum up, typologies of organisations may both provide new ways of looking at individual organisations in which one happens to be interested, and throw light on problems to do with ways of managing them. Two aspects of this search for objective understanding, within which prescriptions tend to be embedded, will be discussed in the concluding sections of this chapter. The first is associations between theories of organisation and prescriptions for management, and the second is the more fundamental issue of connections between theories of organisation and the range of approaches to explanation of the social world dominant at any particular time within the social sciences. A preliminary reference must, however, be made to values as a component of organisational life.

Norms and values

Social workers are likely to draw on organisation theory only in so far as they think it can help them to forward the purposes which they attribute to social work. They are also likely to attribute primarily social work purposes to the organisations in which they are employed, because these are the purposes they think these organisations ought to be serving. To the extent that they do this, their approach may be said to be normative rather than objective, for it expresses a concern to further what they think ought to be, rather than to understand what is. Administrators likewise, as will be discussed in the next chapter, ascribe purposes to organisations, and implement their roles on the basis of their own value judgments on what administration ought to be about, and on the methods which administrators ought to employ. Both social workers and administrators may look to organisation theory not to replace their own ethical judgments, but for the clarification of the nature and significance of value systems as elements of organisational behaviour.

As social psychologists, Katz and Kahn suggest that the bases of organisations as social systems are constituted of role behaviour; of norms as prescriptions for behaviour; and of values as ideological justifications for behaviour. Katz and Kahn stress the integrative significance of these three factors; but unless it is assumed that organisations and individuals have compatible goals, and that organisations are both static and internally homogeneous, they must be acknowledged as sources of conflict also. Whether the emphasis is on consensus or on conflict however, value systems are of interest to the organisation theorist in so far as they influence the behaviour of an organisation's members.

Katz and Kahn refer specifically to system (or organisational as distinct from individual) norms and values, defining these as standards by which behaviour of relevance to the organisation itself is judged. However, the criteria by which members of an organisation judge behaviour within it may be extra-organisational in origin. For example, Gouldner describes a situation in which the norms and values which permeate the life of a community are brought by some of its members into the industrial organisation in which they are employed, and help to determine the form of bureaucratic authority which they are prepared to accept as legitimate.[39] Additionally, Blau and Scott discuss the significance of the co-existence within organisations of bureaucratic and professional orientations: of situations in which the bureaucrat's role performance is based on loyalty to the hierarchy of organisational authority, while the professional employee works to self-imposed standards, derived from reference to the profession rather than to the organisation of which he is temporarily a member.

Such factors as these become directly relevant to daily life if it is accepted that part of the task of managers is to promote the development of norms which, while conducive to organisational effectiveness, will also evoke compliance with organisational authority. Etzioni, adopting an essentially theoretical approach, offers a typology of organisations which includes the notion that control, and compliance with it, may be based on coercion, or on economic incentives, or, in the case of what he describes as 'normative' organisations, on the shared moral commitment of both superiors and subordinates to the organisation's purposes. His thesis is that particular types of control are effective in particular types of organisation; and the identification of the basis, including extra-organisational values, upon which members of an organisation are willing to accept control, thus becomes relevant to the development of an effective system of of authority.

However, while Etzioni as a theorist hypothesises that alternative forms of control are available to organisational *élites*, Etzioni as an individual makes his own moral assertion that reliance on normative control, which acknowledges and respects the values held by individuals, is the most desirable basis of behaviour in organisations.[40]

Values are an element of organisational life which members may bring with them as individuals; or which may be shared by peer groups, or by members of particular sub-systems; or which may 'belong' to the organisation itself to the extent that membership of the organisation demands acceptance of them. The general point to be made in this very brief reference to them is that they are as much a factor to be reckoned with as are technologies or environment or any of the other aspects of organisation which have been identified so far. Both those who exert control, and those whose compliance with it is expected, are confronted by a two-dimensional task: that of identifying and understanding the value systems operating within the organisation, and of deciding how and for what purposes to react to them.

Theoretical perspectives on management

In the case of social workers whose concern is to understand their own occupational environment, an interest in the nature of organisations is likely to be closely linked with an interest in practical problems to do with the ways in which organisations are, or can be, or ought to be managed. At various points in this chapter, discussion of one or other theoretical perspective on organisations has included specific reference to the nature and the problems of management. As, however, the relationship between theories of organisation and prescriptions for management is neither uniform nor static, some particular consideration must be given to the forms which it may take. One set of prescriptions for management was developed when organisation theory was still very young. The 'scientific managers' perceived organisations, both actually and desirably, as formal structures, and workers as most responsive to rigid controls combined with material rewards. Blueprints for management were devised accordingly. The concept of organisation was a very limited one, and as the title ascribed to these early theorists implies, theirs was essentially a 'management point of view'. Although they overlapped in time with each other, the 'human relations' approach constituted a reaction to that of scientific management, and differed from it in fundamental ways. Organisations were comprehended essentially as informal or social structures, and the major researchers and writers were social scientists rather than engineers or practising managers. Nevertheless, there were similarities between the two approaches. First, each focused exclusively upon industrial organisations. Second, each emphasised one particular aspect of organisations. Third, each was directly concerned to provide prescriptions for the 'best' way of managing an organisation. Fourth, organisational and individual needs were assumed to be compatible, and in neither approach was conflict postulated as intrinsic to organisational life. Fifth, as neither approach embodied the idea that organisations may be typed, a prescription for one was a prescription for all.

Both the scientific management and the human relation approaches made their own major and direct contributions to organisation theory and broke the ground for new thinking, and both still continue to influence the practice of management. The concepts of organisation in which they were rooted have, however, changed, and so have the prescriptions for management which are embedded either more or less explicitly in more recent organisation theory.

No longer are studies of organisation restricted to the industrial sector: hospitals, prisons and so on are also part of the field. While organisation theorists search for concepts which may help to clarify the nature of all organisations, it is also recognised that organisations may be typed on the basis of important differences amongst them, and that particular perspectives and concepts may be more relevant to the study of some organisations rather than others. Organisations are recognised as being much more complex than they appeared to be (and possibly were) in the early days of organisation theory: both perceptions of organisations and prescriptions for management which centre on isolated organisational characteristics are suspect. No longer is it assumed that organisational and individual needs are ultimately compatible, or that it is realistic for management to aim at a state of perpetual harmony. The study of organisations has come to include the objective study of management as part of them, rather than being characterised by a preliminary commitment to a management point of view. Particular ways of managing may indeed be perceived as the products of particular types of organisation: a perception deriving from attempts to understand what organisations are actually like and why this is so, rather than from a direct concentration on their problems.

This is not to say that organisation theory is now less relevant than it once was to those whose concern is with how their 'own' organisations can best be run. Rather it is intended to suggest that there has been a significant shift in the ways in which the processes and problems of management are defined. The scientific managers saw management as a form of behaviour which could be imposed upon organisations in accordance with rationally devised and universally relevant prescriptions. Management is now more likely to be perceived as being shaped by, and needing to adjust to, the demands of particular organisational situations. It follows that prescriptions for it need to be both individually devised and rooted in organisation theory of an essentially dynamic kind: textbooks on management which offer sets of golden rules are open to question.

Organisation theory is of some practical use to social workers if it helps them to systematise their thinking about both the trees and the wood of their working situations, and to achieve a more realistic understanding of them. Even this, however, is an unsatisfactorily limited objective for those who wish to make their own moral judgments on these situations, and to attempt to change them. *Ex post facto* explanations of particular organisational structures, or of particular methods of management, as the inevitable products of particular conditions, may help to clarify existing situations, without being of much help to those who wish for change. It is to be remembered that moral judgments on organisational as on other situations require a wider frame of reference than the social sciences have to offer; and commitment to change would seem to require a belief in the possibility of change which the analysis of existing situations may not necessarily foster.

Although organisation theory has expanded beyond an exclusively management-biased stance as its exponents have aimed at greater objectivity, commitment to ethical neutrality is not to be taken for granted. Perrow's attempt to make the sociological theory of organisations relevant for practising managers[41] ends with an exhortation to organisational leaders 'to transcend the technology of administration, and to focus upon such matters as organisational mission and character, and the responsiveness of the inevitably bureaucratic and authoritarian organisation to a presumably democratic society'. Etzioni concludes his comparative study of power and compliance with support for the view that normative rather than coercive compliance ought to characterise the organisational behaviour of the future.[42] These are two examples of opinions about what management ought to be doing which have been openly expressed. Over much of the field, however, it may be more difficult to identify the values which are taken for granted in particular theoretical approaches, or to distinguish between the 'is' and the 'ought' in theories of management: 'one is never sure whether what is being attempted is a description of how organisations actually work, or an abstract discussion of the conditions necessary for their stable functioning.'[43]

One possible bridge between the role of the organisation theorist as a social scientist and that of practising managers, is Gouldner's interpretation of the role of the industrialist sociologist. Gouldner adopts the view that between the realm of what is and the realm of what ought to be, there exists the realm of what can be. It is, in his view, not the job of the sociologist to expatiate upon what ought to be, either by recommending alternative policies or by insisting that some administrative systems are 'better' than others. By dissecting concrete situations, however, sociologists may, according to Gouldner, expose more clearly the complex nature of what is, and therefore of what can be. To this extent, they may help to uncover a variety of solutions to the problems faced by managers, and extend the range of choices open to them. An illustration of this might be that someone in a management position who perceives the organisation only as a formal structure or bureaucracy, or only as composed of people, may be correspondingly limited in his perception of the ways in which, and the directions in which, it could be modified. On the other hand, increased understanding may also call for the acceptance of formerly unacknowledged limitations upon what management can do. For example, the theoretical concept of organisations as open systems may force the conscious acceptance of certain environmentally imposed restraints (such as those embodied in statutorily imposed duties, or the force of public opinion, or the state of the market, or the attitudes of committees or boards) by which freedom of managerial action is limited.

To expect organisation theory to provide direct answers to the problems involved in making organisations work well, is to be doomed to disappointment. Organisation theory is inconclusive, and individual organisations remain unique. Theory may, however, be used to introduce order into one's ways of looking at organisations, and at management as a component process: it may help both to systematise and to extend the range of factors which it is relevant to take into account when specific problems are under consideration.

Organisation theory in social science

Perrow's suggestion, quoted at the head of this chapter, that there are many ways of looking at organisations, may be applied at various levels of generality. Illustrations of some specific ways have constituted the core of the chapter, each of them emphasising certain aspects of organisations to the exclusion of others. Something has also been said about the nature, the advantages and the limitations of dispassionate analysis as distinct from identification with a particular standpoint, such as that of a manager or a social worker. Nothing so far however has suggested the possibility that the ways of looking at organisations which social scientists themselves have to offer, may have their genesis in theories which constitute perspectives not only on organisations, but on social phenomena and institutions in general. This possibility, however, is a very real one.

To begin with, sociological perspectives on organisations may correspond with orientations identifiable throughout the whole sphere of interest of sociology itself. For example, in functionalist terms, social systems are interpreted as being in a continuous process of adjusting to change in order to maintain their equilibrium. Interest centres on the ways in which the parts of a system fit together, in the functions of the parts for the whole, and in the nature of the processes through which the needs of the system in question are met. This approach may be applied to the analysis of any social system: the functionalist will concentrate on problems to do with the sustaining or redefinition of goals, with adaptation, and with the maintenance of solidarity, whether the particular system which interests him is a tribe, or an organisation, or a whole polity.

While the functionalist acknowledges that strain is inherent in any social system because of the incompatibility of the needs of its different parts, the conflict theorist on the other hand postulates conflict itself as the central social phenomenon. Conflict and not the need for integration is the source of change, and power is the most significant determinant of the forms which change takes. Changes in any type of social system, including organisations, are consequently to be analysed in terms of conflicting ends and conflicting interests and the distribution of power.

Each of these two models, presented here in the barest outline possible, is in essence hypothetical. Neither embodies an empirically testable truth; and each is likely to have its ideologically as well as its sociologically committed adherents. Each has strongly influenced the ways in which organisation theorists have approached the analysis both of the nature of organisations and, more specifically, of the roles and the problems of those who manage them. The briefest reflection will reveal something of how significant the selection of one rather than the other of these two particular approaches could be for the way in which the contexts in which work is done are presented.

Another approach is that of the action theorist, who starts from the assumption that social systems do not exist separately from definitions of them by participating individuals. Louis Wirth[44] communicated something of this approach, although long before action theory as such was incorporated into sociology, when he suggested that 'a society is possible in the last analysis because the individuals in it carry around in their heads some picture of that society'. The action theorist focuses on the actors in a situation as both the constructors and the interpreters of reality: an organisation is what its members make it or believe it to be.

The general point which these brief illustrations of sociological perspectives are intended to make, is that affinities may exist between the forms taken by sociological theory in general, and the ways in which sociologists look at organisations. Certain interpretations of the nature of organisations have become possible only at certain stages in the development of sociological theory itself, and this kind of interdependence will persist.

The same is true of psychology, which over time has been the source of equally changing perspectives and interpretations. Here the emphasis is on the behaviour of human beings, whether as members of small groups, as individuals with hierarchies of need to be satisfied, or as occupiers of roles in open systems. On the other hand, the frame of reference used by an economist would emphasise the impact of market situations and of technologies on social institutions, and be likely to incorporate quantitative criteria of efficiency, whether in respect of a social policy or of an organisation.

The use of organisation theory by anyone who wishes to clarify the nature of his own organisational situation seems to call for sensitivity to a number of points. The approaches found within any particular academic discipline should be regarded as neither self-sufficient nor self-contained: the sociologist and the social psychologist alike may perceive organisations as open systems, but each will emphasise different aspects of these systems. Each theoretical approach is only partial: it will reflect an interest in certain questions rather than others. It has to be recognised both that organisation theorists are limited by the paradigms available to them at particular points in time, and that they themselves are selective in the paradigms which they choose to work from. Reliance upon one particular perspective may have the effect of blinding one to the existence of equally illuminating alternatives.

As there is no need to limit oneself to the use of one perspective rather than another, it may also be the case that the different models or perspectives which are available at any one time do not really need to be reconciled with each other. This general point is made by Percy Cohen in the course of a discussion of conflict or consensus models of society: 'it is perfectly possible to conceive of models which would contain some of the predominant characteristics of (the consensus model), and some of those of (the conflict model). In short, it may be possible, and desirable, to construct several models of social systems, rather than only two: this is certainly discomforting to those who think in binary terms'.[45]

If Cohen's point applies to the role of sociologists in the construction of theoretical models, it may also be relevant to social workers in their use of such models. In their case, it would seem important to cultivate an awareness of the theoretical and ideological origins of particular models of organisation, and an appreciation of the idea that while theory evolves from systematic attempts to represent reality, it can never completely encompass it. In a situation in which the most that organisation theory can do is to provide mental constructs which may throw light on certain aspects of reality, it could be argued that laymen as distinct from social scientists may justifiably adopt a pragmatic approach, directed towards the identification of views of organisations which seem most likely to be useful to them in the situations in which they find themselves. Such pragmatism, however, needs to be tempered by the recognition that some theoretical approaches may be more internally consistent than others, some less ideologically biased than others, and some more empirically sub-stantiated than others: the criteria by which a social scientist would evaluate them can be indicative of their validity not only to the theorist but to the layman.

The content of this chapter represents an attempt to illustrate what organisation theory has to offer in the way of insights into the eternally elusive reality of particular organisations. It is a bare skeleton, but a little flesh will be added to it in the form of the discussion of the nature of administration which is to follow.

Chapter four

Administration

The beginning of administrative wisdom is that there is no one best
way of managing an organisation
                                                    T. Burns and G. M. Stalker

Administration is an organisational process which has so far been
mentioned only in passing. Now, supposing that it is possible to decide
upon a working definition, it can be brought into the centre of the
picture.

The *Concise Oxford Dictionary* equates administration with management; and each of these terms has been used so far in this book without
an attempt to distinguish between them. R. G. S. Brown[1] uses
'management' to include 'the formulation of policies, the creation of
machinery for putting them into practice, and the review and appraisal
of what is in fact done', and considers that 'the more conventional term
"administration" is too weak to convey what is involved'. But
'management' is a term which one finds in daily use sometimes as
though management included administration, and sometimes as though
it were part of it. Administration on the other hand may be used
sometimes to refer to the process involved in the formulation of policy
and sometimes to its implementation. It may be used as a synonym
either for the government (an alternative *Oxford Dictionary* definition),
or for the civil service or the staff of Local Authorities who are
employed by government. It may imply routine paper work as distinct
from professional or technical activities; or the 'office' as distinct from
the 'service-delivery' hierarchy of a Social Services department. Processes which in hospitals are described as part of administration, may in
industry be associated with management.

This by no means exhaustive list of possible usages suggests the
futility of trying to find an objective definition of administration upon
which all agree, and which consistently determines the sense in which
the word is used. It thus becomes important both to attempt to

93

understand what is intended by it when it is used by others, and to be clear as to how one is using it oneself. From now on administration will be taken to mean the conscious processes through which organisations are maintained and modified. This definition implies a distinction between activities which are essentially to do with the actual output of goods or the direct delivery of services – such as making the chocolates or treating the patient or visiting the family in need of social work help – and those which derive from the fact that output, whether of goods or of services, requires organisation. Such a definition also implies that administration is a feature of all organisations, army battalions and Family Service Units alike: which is not of course to say that it either does or should or can take the same form in all of them. However, as the presumption in the last chapter was that there are certain characteristics which all organisations share, so now a similar presumption is made in the case of administration.

As a starting point, reference may be made to one particular attempt to identify elements in administration which are shared by organisations in business, social welfare, government, education and medicine; and this will incidentally both reinforce the definition of administration offered above, and include one possible definition of management. J. D. Thompson[2] has suggested that three major functions are performed by the administrative process, whatever the size or complexity of an organisation, and whatever the nature of its output. The first is *direction* which is concerned with what the total organisation is now, but more essentially with its future, and with what it is becoming and should become. The second is *management* which is concerned with the sustenance of the organisation, and which provides the ingredients, the instructions, and the climate which are essential to the organisation's work. The third is *supervision,* which co-ordinates and monitors technical or professional activities, and which governs the utilisation of the resources employed in production.

Thompson considers that there is usually a close correspondence between these three administrative functions and three general levels in an organisation's hierarchy: direction at the top, management in the middle, and supervision at the level of immediate contact with those who are actually making the goods or delivering the services. His concept both of organisations and of administration is thus an essentially hierarchical one, and to this extent limited. As it is possible for organisations to be structured on other than hierarchical bases, it may be useful to dissociate the identification of the functions which their sustenance and development require, from any assumption that these are necessarily correlated with particular levels in a formal structure; or that their implementation is necessarily based on relationships of a superior/subordinate kind. Direction, management, and supervision will thus here be taken to refer to elements in administration, without necessarily implying the inevitability of hierarchical kinds of relationships either amongst those whose responsibilities are purely administrative (or organisational), or between administrators and those who actually 'produce the goods'.

There is one further factor which Thompson's concept of administration does not include, but which must be incorporated into any idea of administration as an essentially organisational activity. This is that a clear-cut distinction cannot always be made between administrative and technical or professional activities. For example, some roles in organisations are essentially administrative in that they are established specifically for the implementation of the functions which Thompson identifies, including supervision of the 'producers'. At the other extreme, some roles such as those of the unskilled workers at a conveyor belt can be clearly excluded. However, some 'producers', such as social workers, who are not administrators in Thompson's sense, may have considerable discretion to choose the ways in which they do the organisation's work. Additionally, as well as being required to work in certain ways rather than others, for organisational rather than professional reasons, they may also actively attempt to modify organisational policies and processes. If social workers are not technically administrators, at least to the extent that they do any of these things they are participants in the total administrative process; and if they wish to influence administrative decisions which affect services to clients, active and positive participation in administration, rather than a simple rejection of 'bureaucracy', may be called for.

To recapitulate, administration is taken to consist of processes which are essentially organisational in character, whether they have to do with the formulation of long-term policies for the organisation as a whole; or with the management of its sub-units; or with the control of the work of the producers; or with the use of discretion by individual producers themselves, either in the implementation of their own roles, or in attempts to influence what goes on in the organisation as a whole or in particular sub-systems within it. Certain positions may be described as administrative because the roles of those who occupy them are primarily organisational rather than directly productive; but only if organisational systems were static, closed, homogeneous, single-purpose and completely bureaucratised, all of which the last chapter suggests that they are not, would it make sense to suggest that administration is an exclusive activity in which some engage and to which others react.

It is primarily for this reason that the discussion of administration which constitutes the rest of this book is addressed directly to social workers, rather than to administrators. As social work roles are shaped by the nature both of social services and of organisations, what social workers can do is also clearly affected by the ways in which organisations are administered, and by the nature of social workers' own participation in, and influence upon, administrative processes. This having been said, and in line with the discussion of the nature of organisations in chapter 3, this chapter will concentrate on an analysis of administration as a process generic to all organisations. Occasional references apart, administration in social work services will be left for special consideration in chapter 5.

It will be well to begin with payment of respect to a warning from Joan Woodward[3] that a 'danger lies in the tendency to teach the principles of administrative wisdom as though they were scientific laws, when they are really little more than administrative expedients found to work well in certain circumstances, but never tested in any systematic way'.

With this in mind, the objective will be not to describe what administrators ought to do but rather, as in the case of organisations, to suggest a frame of reference for considering the nature of the tasks which confront them.

If administration is indeed an organisational activity, it appears logical to start with some consideration of the relevance to it of the nature of organisations, particularly as administrators perceive them. As illustrated in chapter 3, no objective or finite conception of what organisations 'themselves' are like is available, or ever likely to be. Nevertheless, whether they are conscious of it or not, the activities of administrators will be affected by their ideas of what organisations are and ought to be like: 'Does a man live for months or years in a particular position in an organisation, exposed to some streams of communication, shielded from others, without the most profound effect upon what he knows, believes, attends to, hopes, wishes, emphasises, fears and proposes?'[4] If, a Simon[5] suggests, the behaviour of administrators and its effects on others are functions of the organisational situations in which administrators are placed, then there is something to be said for their developing, on the basis of whatever sources of understanding are available, the most systematic and rational ways possible of understanding these situations. In so far as social workers themselves are concerned about the effects of administrative behaviour, and about the ways in which and the purposes for which organisations are or could be used, such understanding is of relevance to them too.

Specific affinities between theories of organisation and prescriptions for managing or, to use the inclusive term, for administering them, have also been illustrated in chapter 3. If the behaviour of administrators is affected by the particular pressures under which they work, it is also likely to be affected by the ways in which they themselves perceive the nature of organisations: perception of an organisation as a bureaucracy will produce administrative behaviour very different in kind from that which derives from a sense of organisations as consisting essentially of people with contributions of their own to make. For reasons such as this, perhaps the most fundamental questions to be asked about the practice of administration have to do with its relationship to ideas about the nature of organisations. If administration is intended to be a rational process in which the decisions made are most likely to produce the intended effects, then perhaps the first task of administrators is to clarify for themselves the particular concepts of organisation they are carrying about in their heads. From this process they may gain at least a more consciously formulated idea of what it is they are administering.

Chapter 3 amounts to an attempt at clarification by one particular individual. It implies that in working with and through organisations, administrators are confronted with the task of taking into account, and weighing in the balance, a range of organisational characteristics which, it is also implied, affect both what they can do and how they should do it. Allowing for the fact that each event is in the last resort unique, the suggestion is that their work involves the management of situations of which major components are the organisational characteristics identified in the course of the chapter. A reiteration of the headings under which the nature of organisations was discussed may serve to make the point: the ideas of bureaucracy, of organisations as processes and as systems, of the co-existence of formal and informal elements, of organisational goals, of people in organisations, of technologies, people and environment, and of value systems in organisations, may serve to provide administrators with a map of the territory within which they have to work. So may the ideas that organisations may be typed, and that methods of administration which might be appropriate to one type are not necessarily best for another. Such conceptual frameworks are tools which may be applied to three distinct administrative tasks: understanding what is, identifying the determinants of what can be, and deciding what ought to be done and why.

All that will be said about administration from now on has its genesis in ideas about the nature of organisations, and in the presumption that administration is essentially an organisational activity. The rest of this chapter constitutes an attempt to identify certain major elements in it, and to consider them under a number of separate headings. The outcome cannot be said to be objective, for others perceive administration differently, and would classify its components accordingly. Each of the elements identified is complex, and all that can be offered is an introductory discussion in each case. However, here is one way into the business of exploring what administration is, or can be, or ought to be about; and the suggestions for further reading at the end of the book are a guide for those who wish to take the exploration further.

Administrative relationships

Beyond the fundamental idea that the purposes and the nature of administration are products of organisations, it is probably impossible to find any one exclusive starting point for an examination of its content. In whatever ways one attempts to dissect administration, in practice its various components have to be synthesised, and no one of them is separable from the others. There are, however, certain concepts which are as central to administration as they are to social work, and in a book intended for social workers, it may make sense to start with one of these.

Administration no less than social work involves relationships. The forms taken by administrative relationships differ from those to be found in social work itself; but although the discussion which follows will emphasise the 'organisational' as distinct from the 'human' aspects of them, the purposes they serve are not dissimilar. Both social work and administrative relationships have to do with the more effective functioning of individuals in social situations.

One way of describing an organisation is as a formal structure of positions throughout which the work to be done is distributed. In order for work to be co-ordinated, the holders of particular positions must relate to others in systematic ways which are mutually understood. As we have seen however, organisations are not simply bureaucracies, and one cannot assume that even the most formal relationships necessary to maintain them can be defined exclusively in bureaucratic terms. The bureaucratic type of relationship, which implies a vertical line of formal authority, may nevertheless be dealt with first.

This is essentially an hierarchical or 'line' relationship between a superior and a subordinate. The superior is responsible for the work of the subordinate and has authority to control what the subordinate does. Correspondingly, the subordinate accepts instructions 'from above'. A line relationship is operating when soldiers accept an order to fire, or when the head of a typing pool distributes work and typists accept it, or when a social worker accepts instructions from a senior that a report on a statutory visit must be written up by such and such a date. Although bureaucratic or line relationships are vertical connections between different 'levels' however, not all of them are rungs in the same ladder. Separate ladders exist in each of a complex organisation's sub-systems. In a factory, for example, as well as a line (or lines) of formal authority from works manager down to operatives, sub-systems such as sales departments, wages departments, typing pools and so on, also depend to some extent upon the operation of their own internal line relationships.

The nature of line relationships once clarified, we can consider their uses. As with other manifestations of bureaucracy, reliance on line relationships may indeed be useful for some purposes rather than others. As well as constituting an authority structure, line relationships form a system of accountability, and of shared responsibility. They may contribute to the clarification of individual roles; and they can provide a basis upon which the activities of members of an organisation, or of sub-systems within it, can be closely controlled, co-ordinated, and supervised. Members of an organisation may feel more secure if they know to whom they are accountable and for what, and what decisions they may make themselves without prior reference upwards. Clarity in line relationships will be helpful on both counts. On the other hand, too much emphasis on the line element in organisational relationships may both restrict personal initiative, and be uncongenial to those whose willing participation, rather than reluctant conformity, is what the organisation needs.

All formal organisation implies the existence of a line, however embryonic; but as no organisation is simply a bureaucracy, neither are line relationships the only basis upon which the members of an organisation may relate formally to each other.

As the reference to sales departments and typing pools and so on implies, not all the work to be done within a complex organisation can be fitted into one vertical line from top to bottom. In particular, certain functions (such as training) are not directly productive, and those who implement them will not slot into a direct hierarchy or line from works manager to bench hand, or from Director of Social Services to social worker. And yet, without some formal authority in relation to certain members of the main hierarchy, they may be unable to do their work. The problem may be overcome by the establishment of specialist positions whose occupants are endowed by their superiors with authority, within the limits of particular policies, to give instructions to the superior's other subordinates. Thus a works manager may endow a training officer with authority to require foremen, in accordance with the firm's training policy, to release apprentices for training for so many hours a week. The training officer's authority over the foremen is limited to the implementation of training policy: he may not instruct them how to manage production within their 'own' departments. This type of relationship, between specialists and their superior's other subordinates, is called a staff relationship: a training officer in a position such as that referred to, may be said to be on the staff of the works manager, or of the Director of Social Services, and to be acting on his behalf.

Yet again, situations may exist in which particular members of an organisation are required to provide a service to others who are authorised to request it: as when the head of a typing pool is required to provide typing services for departmental heads who are authorised to make demands upon these services. The relationship between those requesting a service and those who are expected to provide it is known, not surprisingly, as a service relationship.

Line, staff, and service relationships are not mutually exclusive, and certain positions may require the use of all three. A personnel manager, for example, in addition to being a staff officer responsible for implementing his employer's personnel policy, is at the head of the internal line structure of the personnel department, and is likely to be required to provide a service to other departmental heads seeking to fill vacant positions.

From a number of other possible types of formal relationship[6] one more may be identified here. Situations exist in which people with no formal authority over each other have tasks to perform which require that unless they can accommodate to each other, they have to refer to a joint superior. They may be described as colleagues, and the relationship between them is a collateral one.

The administrative concepts of line, staff, service and collateral relationships may be helpful if they are used to distinguish between some of the different bases upon which formal relationships in organisations can be structured, and to clarify the differing relationships in which members of an organisation may stand with each other. For example, Kogan *et al.*[7] suggest that in hospitals there is confusion when occupants of staff roles are not described or recognised as such, or when individuals are given combinations of tasks, some of which require a staff role and others a line one. It is improbable that such confusion is confined to hospitals; and many training officers in Social Services Departments may feel that they suffer from it.

This categorisation of types of formal relationships is intended to imply that they can be deliberately structured. Administration is not, in this respect, a matter of leaving people to evolve their own working relationships as best they can. Members of organisations do indeed relate to each other as people, and also in certain circumstances as professional peers. But their relationships may be eased, and work be more comfortably and effectively accomplished, if they know where they stand organisationally as well as personally and professionally.

These different kinds of formal relationships may be looked on as devices which are available for use when it seems that they would be helpful. Within small and compact working groups they may not be needed. In large and complex organisations they may be one way, amongst others, of helping people to 'know where they stand'. For the administrator, the problem is to decide, in particular circumstances, how useful it would be to define them.

Authority and its correlates

Any need there may be for establishing formal relationships derives
from the fact that members of an organisation cannot be autonomous
individuals each 'doing his own thing'. Each is a participant in the work
of the organisation as a whole, and administration includes a process
through which the tasks which this work involves are assigned to
individuals; limits are set to what people may do; and arrangements are
made for ensuring that they do what they are supposed to do. If the
process is to be effective, balances have continuously to be sought
between the freedom which individuals may need if they are to do their
particular part of the organisation's work well, and the restraints, the
checks and the controls without which the incorporation of individual
performances into a combined operation would be impossible. Administrative relationships of the kind which have just been discussed are
arrangements for permitting or requiring some people to control the
behaviour of others; for making some people accountable to others; for
ensuring that holders of particular positions have the jurisdiction they
need if they are to function effectively; for requiring some people to
provide services to others; and so on. They constitute a formal system
of authority.

Authority, like relationships, is a concept familiar to social workers.
It is impossible to take an analysis of the nature of administration very
far without being confronted by it, and indeed references to it have
already been unavoidable in the discussion of administrative relationships so far. It has, however, many faces, and its nature in administration cannot be examined without reference to other concepts such as
discretion and responsibility, which are perhaps more congenial to
social workers who are concerned about their own organisational
positions. Moreover, although the following discussion emerges directly
out of a discussion of formal administrative relationships, bureaucratic
authority will appear as only one of the types of authority relationship
upon which organisational life depends.

It is necessary first of all to define authority, and it may be useful to
do this by distinguishing it from power. Power is simply the ability to
act in a particular way and to produce particular effects. It is in essence
the product of personality used at will, and it does not imply that the
action taken is legitimate. Power cannot be delegated, and individuals
cannot be invested with it: either they have it, or they do not. Even the
head of an organisation may be without power, if he lacks knowledge
or skill or personality; or he may exercise power unduly if the nature of
his personality is such that people do what he says because they are
afraid to do otherwise.

Authority on the other hand implies the existence of a right to be
obeyed, which is acknowledged by those over whom the authority is

intended to be exercised. Unlike power, which is personal, it can be delegated to others. It incorporates the right to make decisions, and is thus essential for the implementation of all but routine tasks. Throughout organisational systems, administrators retain some decision-making rights for themselves, and delegate others to the points at which they are needed if work is to be effectively done.

The distinction between authority and power is an important one in practice, both for administrators and for those whose behaviour they wish to influence; and perhaps for moral as well as pragmatic reasons. Ought people in organisations to be obeyed because they are personally powerful, or because they are vested with authority? When contrasted with power, and especially with power irresponsibly used, authority may appear in a more positive light than expected.

One type of authority may be delegated to positions rather than to individuals: the right to make particular decisions is then the accepted prerogative of whoever occupies a particular position at a particular time. This kind of authority is essentially bureaucratic; and so is that which derives from written rules, whether internal to the organisation or in the form of the statutory rules and regulations which impose duties upon Local Authorities. Like other manifestations of bureaucracy, each of these types of authority may be useful for some purposes and not for others.

Official positions and written regulations are not, however, the only possible sources of authority within an organisation. Authority may be accorded downwards, upwards and laterally to individuals, as distinct from 'office holders', either because of their competence or expertise, or because they are respected as persons. For example, positional authority delegated to a staff officer by his superior may be clearly defined, but unless the staff officer is professionally competent, the authority which he needs to be accorded by those with whom he does his daily work may not be available to him. Additionally, they are more likely to invest him with authority if they respect him as a person.

The idea that authority in organisations has various sources, and that in order to be effective it must be accorded, gives rise to questions about the bases upon which individuals are prepared to invest others with it. They may comply with another's authority on any of the grounds just mentioned: because they accept what the regulations say, or because they attach authority to a particular position or 'office', or because they respect an individual office-holder's competence or his person. To varying degrees, discretion is available to administrators to decide upon the type of authority upon which to rely. Etzioni's idea of a correlation between particular types of organisation and the types of control with which people are willing to comply (see p. 85) provides a basis for a general approach. In the specific situations of daily life, the administrator will have to walk his own official/professional/personal tightrope.

If one correlate of the authority of one person is the compliance of another, so authority in organisations must be perceived as embodying responsibility. Authority and responsibility are also to be correlated with each other in so far as the person to whom authority is delegated assumes responsibility for the use of it. But there is more to it than this: for even when in a line relationship the subordinate assumes responsibility for the use of the authority delegated to him, the superior cannot free himself of the responsibility for having delegated it, and for what subsequently happens. This is perhaps one of the reasons for reluctance to delegate authority, and for further reluctance to 'let go' even when a formal decision to delegate has been made. Responsibility, moreover, is in the last resort essentially personal: it cannot be defined in exclusively organisational terms. In whatever position I hold, what I do with the authority at my disposal, whether I delegate it or not, is a personal responsibility of which I cannot be rid.

For this reason, amongst others, it seems important to distinguish between responsibility and accountability. If responsibility is personal, accountability is organisational. It has to do with control. If a line constitutes a system through which authority is delegated, it is also a system through which members of an organisation can be called to account for what they do.

An illustration of ways in which personal responsibility and administrative accountability may be built in to the structure of organisations (or parts of them) is given by Susser and Watson[8] in the course of a discussion of medicine and bureaucracy in hospitals. They describe how the personal, professional and legal responsibility of all qualified and registered doctors is identical, regardless of their positions. Nurses, however, are in a very different situation. Although the behaviour of nurses is a professional matter, and rules of conduct for all nurses are laid down by their professional associations within a hospital what each nurse must or may do is defined by her position in a formal hierarchy of accountability which rises from (under the old nomenclature) probationer to matron. Certainly the responsibilities which those who call themselves professional people consider themselves to carry do not all derive from the positions which they hold in particular organisations; but they are in varying degrees modified by them. In a Local Authority Social Services Department, the felt personal responsibility of the social worker for providing a professional service to, for example, children in care, has to find expression within an administrative accountability system. This links the social worker with the Director, who in his turn can be called to account by the Social Services Committee, acting on behalf of the Local Authority whose formal duty it is to provide the service, if the care of an individual child goes radically wrong. Because they are members of such organisations, social workers are held to be accountable, as well as feeling themselves to be responsible, for what they do.

If members of an organisation are to be held accountable for their performance, however, justice demands that certain conditions to do with the delegation of authority hold good. The first is that the authority delegated to them is reasonably clearly defined and that they are helped to understand the limits within which they are free to use their own discretion. Second, they must be able to feel that the authority vested in them is real: that they are trusted to 'get on with it' without feeling that a superior is hanging on to the controls himself. Third, the authority delegated must be commensurate with the requirements of the work to be done: no one can do a job unless he is free to take the decisions which it needs. As, however, no areas of authority can be so clearly defined as to encompass all the decisions which work requires, a corollary of the effective delegations of authority is a sensitivity on the part of those in whom it is vested, to the situations in which it is important to refer upwards to a superior for advice, information or instruction. The need for this sensitivity is in itself an example of the administrative responsibility even of those who may not themselves be administrators.

Authority has been discussed as a phenomenon without the use and deployment of which organisational life would be impossible. Unlike authoritarianism, which implies a value commitment to obedience to authority as opposed to individual liberty, the concept of authority is itself neutral: it is the ways in which authority is distributed and used in practice which one may judge good or bad, productive or unproductive. Administrators have authority, of different types, at their disposal. They have to decide how to use it; and in particular how to delegate it. The delegation of authority by superiors is a way of distributing work. It is a means whereby available skills may be more fully used, and which may liberate individuals to use their discretion and to assume responsibility. This they may welcome; or it may possibly place too heavy a load upon them. Unlike power, authority implies the co-operative acceptance of it by those upon whom the exercise of it impinges; and it has personal as well as organisational origins and implications. It is not necessarily bureaucratic in nature, although for either good or ill it may be. It may be used to hold an organisation, or parts of it, tightly together, with the emphasis on control from the top and upon accountability; or it may be deployed to create an organisation in which authority, as distinct from power, is an attribute of the 'front-line', or of experts rather than office holders.

The use of authority in administration does not imply that all the behaviour of subordinates is governed by it: they may happen to agree with a superior, and act out of personal conviction, rather than in response to his authority. Nor does it mean that any one individual accepts the authority of only one other: he may, for example, accept the authority of one person as to what the regulations say, and that of another as to what, this being the case, he ought to do. What the use of authority can do is to promote the co-ordination of individual activities; distribute the right to make decisions to the individuals who have the particular knowledge and skills which these decisions require; and provide the basis of a system through which individuals can be held accountable for what they do.

Administrative relationships and authority structures constitute the formal framework within which the work of an organisation is done. Wilfred Brown[9] takes the view that the more formal an organisation 'the more clearly we will know the bounds of discretion which we are authorised to use . . .'. Burns and Stalker[10] on the other hand emphasise, on the basis of empirical research, that formal structures are not the only framework within which work can be effectively organised on a day-to-day basis. In certain conditions and for certain purposes flexibility, and reliance on a 'network' rather than a 'hierarchy' of authority and control, may be more appropriate methods of administration. A point embedded in each point of view is that organisational structures need not just happen, but can be consciously created. The task of the administrator in this respect is to attempt to create an organisation, or perhaps a sub-unit of one, which he thinks is appropriate to the work to be done and the people who are available to do it.

Work and resources

The primary purpose of organisation is the accomplishment of work which cannot be done except when the activities of individuals are co-ordinated with each other. The performance of this work also involves both the recruitment of resources, and their deployment. On this basis, administration is a process of organising resources to get work done.

Loosely, the work of an organisation may be said to consist of the tasks which have to be done if organisational purposes or goals are to be served. But as we have already seen (pp. 80–1), an organisation's goals cannot be objectively defined; and the real as distinct from the intended work of an organisation is that which is actually done by individual members of it. Thompson associates work of an administrative kind (that which is intended to promote production) with particular levels in an organisational hierarchy. For him, work at the top consists of deciding the nature of the tasks to which the activities of the whole enterprise are to be applied, of recruiting resources, and of directing the organisation into the future. In the 'middle', it has to do with implementing the pursuit of objectives determined from above. At supervisory level it involves the co-ordination and the control of the technical or professional activities of those whose work it is to produce the output, whether of goods or of services. Thompson's perception of the distribution of work amongst administrators implies that it is essentially a function of particular positions within a formal and hierarchical structure.

Burns's and Stalker's concept of organic systems of management, however, embodies the view that such formal role-definitions are neither essential components of organisations, nor always the most useful method of distributing work. It implies that work need not be allocated formally to particular positions, and that the work done by individuals may be allowed to be determined by what they have to offer in the way of the knowledge and skills which particular situations happen to require. It may be useful to supplement this idea with Wilfred Brown's[11] notion that work in organisations consists of two major components: 'the prescribed components – those things that the person in the role must do; and the discretionary components of work – those decisions or choices that the person in the role must make'. The administrator who delegates authority is in fact endowing others with the discretion to decide how to implement their roles: which is to say how to do 'their' bit of the organisation's work, whether this is administrative or productive. Administration thus involves the making of decisions about what work is to be done, how it is to be done, and by whom.

But the nature of the work to be done within an organisation is not determined exclusively on an internal basis. First, there is the matter of organisations as open systems interacting with an environment, upon which they are in varying ways dependent for sanctions for what they do, for instructions, and for resources. From a 'work' point of view, an organisation may be perceived as an intake/throughput/output system. It takes in instructions and resources, and works upon them to produce the goods or services which justify its existence. Those who are employed within an organisation may have to accept certain overriding external definitions of their work as major determinants of the daily tasks to be done. The work of industrial organisations is modified by changes in market situations; that of statutory social service organisations by changes in legislation; that of Colleges of Education by changes in national policies for higher education; and so on.

Second, there is the significance of technologies, or of professional expertise and values, as determinants of the nature of productive work, of the ways in which it can or perhaps has to be done, and of the ways in which its performers think it ought to be done. With specific reference to industrial organisations, Wilfrid Brown[12] stresses the need for managers to understand the nature and significance of technical change: only by *understanding* can managers have a mastery of the situation. If they do not understand, the situation masters them instead. As will be suggested in the conclusion to this chapter, the administration of organisations in which the producers include professionals, seems to call for an understanding by administrators of the ways in which those professionals wish to interpret the nature of the work which their organisational roles embody.

To sum up, an organisation is a means of doing work, and administration includes the process of defining the work to be done, and of distributing it. This distribution may be specific and formal, and to particular positions; but it may also emerge from the skills and the knowledge which individuals are given the opportunity to contribute to the solution of particular problems. In any role, there is both a compulsory and a discretionary element; and the delegation of authority is a process which affects the latitude available to individuals to define for themselves the work which they do. Administrators are required to discriminate between what must be done and what may be done, and to decide how specifically roles should be defined. Moreover, the work to be done by an organisation as a 'collective' is determined by external as well as internal factors, such as instructions from the environment, and the changing nature of the technological or professional processes which output involves.

At various points, reference has been made to distinctions between administration and work which is directly productive. At the same time, certain productive roles may allow, or indeed call for, participation by their occupants in activities which are aimed at modifying the work done throughout the sub-systems of which those roles are a part, or indeed that of the organisation as a whole. Once professionals are employed in organisations they assume roles which, although to varying degrees and in varying ways, are defined by the organisation. Even to the extent that the compulsory element in their roles is modified by a discretionary one, their work is not only personal, professional and directly productive, but also organisational, in so far as it includes the task of influencing the decisions made by those whose roles are administrative ones.

The resources available to an organisation are one major determinant of the work which can be done. The work which is done is a function of the uses to which available resources are put. In some circumstances, the problem may be how to cut down resources as a consequence of a reduction in the amount of work to be done; but in the administration of social services, it seems reasonable to take it that the predominant problem is that of scarcity of resources in relation to unlimited demand. The administrative task thus involves both the recruitment of resources, and their deployment between competing uses.

This task is central to administration, whether at the top of an organisation, or at any other position of administrative authority. The major concern of the head of an organisation must be to recruit resources for the work of an organisation as a whole. In doing this, he works outside the formal organisation itself, for resources have to be recruited through and from the super-systems to which that organisation is connected: such as the money market in the case of industrial organisations, and the system of local government in the case of Local Authority Social Services Departments. The need for resources may likewise derive from external pressures which cannot be internally controlled. For example, the work which must be done within a particular factory, and the resources necessary for doing it, may be defined in a distant country, and in the case of social service organisations the influential factors will include changes in legislation, or in the policies of local or central government. At the same time, demands for resources will be expressed from within the formal organisation itself, and its head has to decide how to respond to pleas for additional resources, brought to bear upon him from within the system of which he is the representative to those who control the supply. These controllers may themselves be operating in conditions of scarcity, be facing competing demands upon them, and have different priorities to take into account in deciding how the resources they control are to be deployed. The Maud Committee[13] made this point in respect of Local Authorities in 1967: 'There is a lamentable disparity between the financial responsibilities of local authorities and the taxable resources allocated to them. Their development is thus greatly influenced, and in many directions determined, by the government grants available'. The point hardly needs remaking in the situation in which economic conditions and government economic policy places Local Authorities a decade or so later.

The position and the role of a Director of Social Services in such a situation illustrate perhaps more clearly than does anything else the open, public and political, as distinct from the bureaucratic or even the professional, nature of the organisations in which social workers may have to implement their roles. It may perhaps also serve to illustrate the significance of the formal position allocated in legislation to heads of departments within the formal structure of local government, for this can be an important determinant of their ability to compete for resources.

Competition for resources is one side of the coin, of which the allocation of resources is the other. Within the limits set by external allocators, the head of an organisation has both discretion to decide upon the uses to which all available resources are to be put, and authority to delegate immediate control over them throughout the organisation's membership. To this extent, delegated authority within an organisation incorporates the right to decide how to use resources.

Emphasis has so far been placed on the role of the 'top' administrator, both outside the formal organisation and within it. But both the recruitment and the deployment of resources are intrinsic to the implementation of any other administrative role as well. To the extent that they control resources, industrial foremen and team leaders in social work alike must decide directly how those resources can best be deployed, or how the authority to deploy them is to be delegated. They must also argue the case, as they see it, for increased resources for that part of the organisation's work for which they are administratively accountable, or for which they assume responsibility. This again is an unbureaucratic concept of administration. The administrator is not there simply, or even primarily, to instruct or to control, but both as a recruiter and as a deployer of the resources upon which productive work depends.

But what are these resources? Money is clearly the basic resource; but it is not a working resource until it has been used to buy material equipment, or human skills, or the time in the form of man hours which the performance of work requires. Moreover, those who control the supply of money may not be willing to make money available until they are positively convinced about the uses to which it is to be put. Budgeting is thus a process of estimating the cost of the resources needed to maintain particular operations or to develop or add to them, and of formulating plans and translating them into fiscal terms.[14] At every point, the case for money to be made available has to be made on the basis of what the money is needed for. At the same time, the administrator seeking to recruit material or human resources or the money with which to buy them will wish to retain as much discretion as he can to decide how, once obtained, they are to be deployed. He will want them with as few strings attached as possible.

Generalisations are sometimes made about the balance between 'material' and 'human' resources in different types of enterprise. The steel industry has become increasingly capital intensive, and one of its major current problems is the over-availability of man-power. The resources of the family doctor services on the other hand are to a very large extent indeed in the form of the knowledge and skills of the doctors themselves. What of the organisations within which social workers are employed?

The work of a Family Service Unit consists of the social work service offered by social workers to clients and, as are those of a child guidance clinic, its resources are essentially human. At the other end of this particular spectrum are Local Authority Social Services Departments, providing not only the ministrations of social workers and their colleagues, but residential and day care accommodation requiring the maintenance and development of massive and complex capital programmes. Without such capital resources the use of the 'human' resources of these organisations would be crippled.

The balance to be maintained between human and other resources in the implementation of Local Authority services is, however, not a matter which can be determined either departmentally or even within the formal structure of the Local Authority itself. The money to buy different kinds of resources has to be recruited through different types of public financing, and at both local and national levels of government. This illustrates once again the significance of the nature of organisations as open-systems, linked to and dependent upon behaviour in the super-systems within which limits are set to what they can do.

The general points made so far may be summarised as follows. Administration in any type of organisation involves the organisation of resources to get work done. This implies both the recruitment of resources and their deployment; and their deployment entails the delegation throughout the organisation of authority to decide how they are to be used. The total resources of an organisation have to be recruited from outside, but internally the task of recruiting them for particular sub-systems is a matter for administrators at every level. The basic resource is money, which is used to buy capital or other material equipment, or knowledge and skills, or time; and organisations vary both in the balance between these different kinds of resource, and in the types of super-systems within which and through which resources have to be recruited.

The resource function of administration in organisations in which the major productive process is social work will be discussed in chapter 5, but one further general point may be made here, about administration in conditions of scarcity.

If resources are scarce, the problem can be tackled in more than one way. Greater effort can be put into attempts to recruit more resources; or output can be deliberately cut; or attention can be given to developing ways in which existing resources can be more efficiently used. These three approaches are clearly not mutually exclusive, and the administrator faces the problem of deciding what is most needed in particular circumstances, what is possible, and how it is to be achieved. He may find himself in a situation in which the recruitment of extra resources from outside is not feasible, and in which there can be no easing of pressure without recourse to other methods.

The concept of rationing, as a means of limiting work to what can be managed with existing resources, serves to illustrate the general idea that administration is to do with making 'what goes on' in organisations more rational, in the sense of being deliberately determined and consciously controlled. In situations in which demand is unlimited and resources are therefore scarce, the use of rationing devices cannot be avoided. These can, however, be either covert and unsystematic or, to some degree at least, open and deliberately constructed.

In a discussion of supply and demand in the NHS, Enoch Powell[15] asserted that 'the worse kind of rationing is that which is unacknowledged; for it is the essence of a good rationing system to be intelligible and consciously accepted'. He argues that in the hospital service waiting lists are regarded as symptomatic of inadequate resources, but that the professions involved are less willing to acknowledge them as a covert and frequently arbitrary form of rationing which protects the hospitals from overloads of work. Roy Parker[16] introduces a discussion of scarcity in social services by emphasising the infinity of need as well as of demand. Like Enoch Powell, he takes the view that if rationing is not conscious and explicit, and if it does not occur before the service is actually offered, demand will in any case be controlled by the emergence by default of one form of rationing or another. Such rationing may take the form of deterrence, in which the conditions accompanying the receipt of the service are so unattractive that people are discouraged from applying; or of deflection of demand to another organisation; or of delay in providing the service so that potential users just 'give up'; or of allowing people to misunderstand the nature of the services for which they may apply, or to remain in ignorance of their existence. Professor Parker concludes with the assertion that 'one of the principal tasks of chief officers, committees or board of governors is to fight for additional resources. But, however successful they may be in this, they also have the task of deciding the main rationing procedures which will be adopted in the services for which they are responsible. This is a matter of policy'. If it is a matter of policy, it is by definition also a matter of conscious choice.

An accompaniment of the conscious rationing of demand, or an alternative to it, can be dilution: an attempt to do more with the same resources by spreading them more broadly. The outcome of this may be a drop in standards, and the choice may have to be made between providing a better service to fewer people, or a less good service to more. Dilution clearly involves a redeployment of resources: but it is not necessarily the only form of redeployment possible in conditions of scarcity. An alternative is to attempt to ensure that existing resources are more efficiently used.

Redefinitions of the work to be done and the establishment of priorities; reallocation of work so that skills can be used to better purposes; and the reorganisation of tasks so that time can be saved, are ways of husbanding resources which conditions of comparative plenty do not tend to inspire. To this extent, scarcity may sometimes be the mother of efficiency.

Efficiency, like bureaucracy and indeed like administration, sounds cold to professional ears. If, however, it is defined as the ratio of useful work done to the resources expended on it, then it is as important in professional activity as in work of any other sort. The criteria of efficiency used by professionals will differ from bureaucratic ones; but so long as administrators are concerned to promote the work of an organisation, rather than seeing the organisation as an end in itself, their search for greater efficiency can be directed towards professional rather than bureaucratic purposes.

In the end, administration can be summed up in one phrase as the process of organising resources to get work done. All the other aspects of it discussed in this chapter are probably most usefully to be seen as instrumental to this central purpose.

Communication

A creative view of administration would be that through leadership and the provision of support, as well as through the exercise of authority of one kind or another, administrators provide the backing which the performance of the organisation's work requires. Administrators are not themselves on the 'production line'. Rather it is their job to see that output is produced by others and that, in so far as this is feasible the organisation functions as a co-operative enterprise.

No co-operation, and thus no organisation, is possible without communication, which it thus becomes the administrator's task to facilitate. In Chester Barnard's[17] view indeed, the main administrative task is to develop and maintain a system of communication. Barnard considered that this demands first the definition of organisational positions, and second, the recruitment to these positions of people whose skills include the capacity to expand the means of communication on an informal basis. Thus he sees communication, like other aspects of organisation, as having both formal and informal aspects.

Formally, the structure of an organisation constitutes not only an authority system, but a communications system. Embryonic though this system may be, it is the framework within which or in relation to which the much more complex networks of communication which the day-to-day implementation of particular roles requires must be developed. Those who need to communicate with each other are not simply 'people', but the occupants of roles of which the content may remain substantially constant, whoever the current occupants may be. In so far as formal structures make communication between the occupants of given positions either easier or more difficult, the creation and maintenance of helpful ones is indeed a basic administrative task. This is the case whether the administrator in question is at the very top of the organisation, or responsible for the functioning of a sub-unit of it.

In scientific management theory, concepts of communication were essentially hierarchical. The 'line' was a communication system down which orders from the top were passed. A modification of this view was that it was also a channel through which information necessary for wise top-level decision-making could be filtered upwards. Once organisations came to be analysed as social systems, the existence of informal or inter-personal (as distinct from inter-positional) communication began to attract attention. Organisational psychologists were concerned to understand it, and management theorists to explore its potential significance. At the other extreme from the viewpoint of scientific management, is the concept which Burns and Stalker[18] incorporate into their notion of 'organic' management: 'Nothing should inhibit individuals from applying to others for information and advice, or for additional effort'. This is as much as to say that in so far as the performance of the work in hand requires it, everyone should feel that he has access to everyone else.

Administrators need to understand what they can of the forms which communication within and between organisations can take, and to adopt prescriptions for developing it which seem to be appropriate to particular situations. Neither more formal and closed, nor more informal and open, methods of communication can be judged as being good or bad in themselves. They have to be evaluated on the basis of their appropriateness for the specific purposes which are being aimed at.

Communication is inherent in any human interaction, and is in this respect limitless; but the administrator's interest in it must have some boundaries. In any particular administrative position, which is by definition a point in a communication system, the proper subject matter of communication is what the administrator needs to know himself, and what he considers that others need to know, if the work for which he is responsible is to be well done. He must be both the recipient of communications, and the channeller of them – whether up, down, or laterally – to the positions at which he thinks their content is needed.

The substance of communication may be factual information, or ideas or emotions or attitudes. The methods may be, in considerable variety, face-to-face, or oral, or written, each of them with varying degrees of formality or informality, or of individuality or imper-sonality. The purposes may be to transfer or to elicit information, or to facilitate decision-making, or to exercise control, or to exert influence, or to encourage participation.

In sum, communication in organisations is so infinitely complex a process, that little can be done in the space available here except to say so.[19] In administration, however, perhaps the first task is to become consciously aware of it as an element in organisational life which requires constant and deliberate attention. The administrator must be continuously asking himself what there is in what he is currently doing that should be communicated elsewhere. What to communicate, and why and when and how and to whom, are questions which are appropriately constantly in mind. The problems of how to be open to receive communications from others, and of how to respond to them, are of corresponding significance. Moreover, as work in cases of actual or potential non-accidental injury to children may serve to illustrate, communication in an organisational sense is a matter for social workers as well as for administrators. In such cases, they are not autonomous individuals acting in a professional capacity: they are members of organisations, and their responsibility for participation in effective communication is as much of an administrative organisational kind as it is professional.

Planning

As we have seen, it is possible to define administration as the process of implementing policies received 'from above'. If, however, administrators have any discretion at all at their disposal, this definition is imperfect, for in using their discretion they inevitably put their own stamp on situations. Their activities modify existing policies, and within their jurisdictions they can create policies of their own. Such a definition also implies a very passive rather than a potentially creative concept of administration. Much more positively, administration can be seen as a process which is concerned not only with the present, but with the future. Thompson associates this 'directing' function particularly with the 'top' of the hierarchy. Helen Montgomery[20] likewise suggests that a major concern of the 'top' administrator must be to develop a capacity to see the organisation within an historical context, and not only as it is, but as what it is to become. Such responsibility for future developments, however, need surely not be restricted to those at the top whose concern is with the formal organisation as a whole. Within the limits of their own authority, those whom Thompson would call managers and supervisors also have scope for shaping the future of their own sub-systems, and for bringing pressures to bear upwards, as well as for deciding how existing situations can best be organised.

In so far as this is indeed the case, planning is a two-dimensional activity for all participants in the administrative process. It implies both the formulation of operating plans to do with the rational application of existing resources to existing work, and the development of intentions for the future.

The time-scales of planning run from a day-to-day basis to periods which may extend so far into the future, that the circumstances in which plans as originally made will come to fruition can be predicted only with considerable uncertainty. The length of the overall time-span available for longer-term planning is as likely as not to be determined outside the formal organisation itself, in the super-system upon which it is dependent. Thus, for example, until the economic uncertainties of the 1970s, universities were financed on a quinquennial basis and had considerable, and highly valued, freedom to plan major developments on a five-year scale. Social services departments, on the other hand, are constrained by the system of annual estimates which characterise the financial structure of local government. Internally, it is frequently assumed, the time-scale to which administrators work lengthens as they move up the hierarchy. It may, however, be unwise to take this assertion as axiomatic as the two following examples illustrate.

First, there is a distinction to be made between the location of ultimate responsibility for long-term planning for the organisation 'as a whole', and the actual process through which long-term plans are developed. The head of an organisation may be said to be responsible for overall planning, and much of his work may consist of the formulation of long-term developments. At the same time, discretion is available to him to decide how and when, or whether or not, to involve others in the planning process. Furthermore, overall responsibility for long-term planning need not always be vested in one particular position. For example, the Vice Chancellor who is the titular administrative head of a university is *primus inter pares* in relation to the Senate; and the Senate is the academic (or professional) body in which a corporate responsibility for planning the future development of a university is vested.

Second (as the above example also illustrates), planning of a long-term kind is not a function exclusively of those whose roles are primarily administrative. Nor is it a matter of concern only to those at the top of the administrative hierarchy. On a microscopic, as distinct from a macroscopic scale, it can be argued that social workers themselves should be planners; and the futures to which they need to look may be further ahead than any which a Director of Social Services may have in mind. Thus Roy Parker[21] stresses the need for planning for children in long-term care. There should, he suggests, be 'a recognisable plan at any point in time for each child, and this plan should be flexible enough to be adapted to new knowledge, new situations, and not least to the child's own preferences'. Whatever the social worker's responsibility, however, this kind of planning is not an activity which can be contained within exclusively professional roles. Professor Parker emphasises the significance of the inter-connection between the plans which social workers may make, or may wish to make, for individual children, and the planning which goes on elsewhere in the organisation:

The case for planning for individual children is connected with the

115

more general planning which any organisation must undertake. Planning, that is, which is represented by estimates, capital programmes, staff training schemes and such like. It is by no means clear exactly what this relationship is but it plainly exists. Under present circumstances these general plans are dominant and represent one of the permanent features in the environment in which plans for individual children must be formulated. With a clearer view of what it is hoped to achieve for individual children in care, a better balance may be struck in which specific plans in part *determine* the overall planning procedures.

Planning, at whatever organisational level, and whatever the time-scale, implies selecting objectives and finding ways of working towards them: it involves choosing between alternative objectives, and alternative procedures. Each choice of an alternative involves reaching a conclusion about a situation, which is to say making a decision about what is or is not to be done.

If a decision is defined simply as something which precedes action, the concept is so trivial as to be in no way useful. As P. H. Levin[22] suggests, 'it does not do justice to the complexity of the processes by which governments and organisations make decisions. It does not, for example, afford us any means of describing what goes on during the often lengthy period separating the first awareness of the need for a decision and the decision itself, and the further lengthy period separating decision and action'. Levin develops the concept to the point of suggesting that a decision can be more distinctively defined as a deliberate act, either individual or collective, which generates commitment on the part of the actor or actors, to a reasonably specific course of action. A decision is thus by definition always consciously made, and of such significance as to lead its makers to take consequential actions.

On the basis of this definition, decision-making seems to justify being attributed with a central function in administration. H. A. Simon[23] perceives administration as essentially a decision-making process, and his interest in it as such is concentrated on questions about the nature of rational choice. For Simon, rationality is perhaps the most highly valued element in administrative behaviour: 'the correctness of an administrative decision is a relative matter – it is correct if it selects appropriate means to reach designated ends. The rational administrator is concerned with the selection of these effective means'. If, however, it is accepted that administration cannot be clearly separated from policy-making, administrators are involved in selecting not only means, but ends. Their decision-making therefore cannot be exclusively a matter of engineering, but involves also the making of value choices, the rightness or wrongness of which is not quantifiable. Simon indeed suggests that the distinction between factual elements and value elements in decision-making, provides a basis for making a distinction between questions of 'administration' and questions of 'policy'.[24] Some decisions taken in organisations may be judged good or bad in the sense of being effective or otherwise in relation to agreed ends. Others, which have involved the choice of ends, can be subjected only to value judgments. Nevertheless, they too may be either more or less rational, in the sense of being more or less internally consistent, or compatible with each other.

Like planning, decision-making is a matter both of the present and of the future, and of varying time-scales. Decisions have to be made about what is to be done today, and about developments which may take years to mature. But in any case, decisions made on a matter immediately in hand are possible determinants of the decisions which can be made in the future: they may make certain future decisions possible, or they may do the reverse. The consideration of the possible indirect consequences of apparently short-term decisions is thus a critically important aspect of administrative activity.

Equally important are the processes through which the decisions which administrators take are arrived at. Within limits, administrators are vested with authority to make decisions: which indeed is what the delegation of authority means. There are decisions which can be made only by the holders of particular positions, and the support which administrators give to producers may consist, to a considerable extent, of their willingness to make such decisions. These are not personal decisions but rather organisational, in the sense of being made by the holders of positions rather than by individuals acting in their own right. They may, however, be made either autonomously, or as the outcome of a participatory process in which those who have something useful to contribute, or who stand to be affected by them, have been involved. Thus decisions may be *taken* by administrators, but the *making* of those decisions can be, to varying degrees, a democratic and co-operative activity.

Planning, decision-making and decision-taking are active ingredients of administration, requiring that one eye be kept on the present, and the other on the future. They constitute conscious attempts to control the course of events, through the making of choices between alternatives, both of means and of ends, and by directing behaviour towards consciously chosen objectives.

Personnel management

So far, this discussion of administration has been deliberately concentrated on abstract and impersonal concepts: administrative relationships, authority, work and resources, communication, planning and decision-making. The intention has been to emphasise yet again that organisations and administration are not simply a matter of personalities. At the same time, it is only people and not organisations who can act; it is people who occupy positions in organisations; and it is people who produce the output. The work of recruiting, deploying and keeping people must therefore be incorporated into the roles of those upon whose supportive activities the maintenance and development of an organisation depend.

In organisations where this work is allocated to specialists, it constitutes the core of the activity called personnel management; and this seems a convenient title under which to discuss it, whether it is done by specialists, or incorporated into other administrative roles.

The origins of personnel management can be traced back to the attempts of enlightened nineteenth-century employers to improve the lot of their workers. Philanthropy, however, is no longer considered an adequate justification for, or explanation of, industrial employers' concern with working conditions. Cuming's[25] interpretation of the history of such concern implies the gradual disappearance of paternalism, and seems to offer a more realistic guide to the underlying philosophy of industrial personnel management:

> ... there has been nothing altruistic about the ways in which personnel management has developed. Innovations have tended to be based on the assumption that what is good for the individual is good for the organisation as well. Each step forward can be seen as an investment to enhance the contribution, and thus the value, of the labour force, with the ultimate aim of enabling each individual to see that his interests and those of the organisation for which he works are the same.

The idea that employees' welfare is to be a matter of concern for organisational reasons rather than as an end in itself is open to question on moral grounds; and the notion that the interests of organisation and individuals are necessarily the same seems to be an oversimplification of reality. Nevertheless, whatever the philosophy by which individual participants in the personnel management function would wish to justify their activities and their methods, recruiting, deploying and keeping workers appears on a common sense basis alone to be an inescapable administrative function in any organisation. Specialists may or may not be needed; but a breakdown of personnel management into the functions typically assigned to it, suggests the existence of matters which require attention whoever in a particular organisation, or perhaps in its super-systems, may be given, or assume, responsibility for them.

Cuming suggests that the scope of personnel management includes the functions of employment, training and education, wages and salaries, industrial relations, and welfare and safety. The extent to which each of these is a matter to be managed internally in social work services will clearly vary considerably. An autonomous voluntary organisation may appropriately assume an employer's responsibility for them all. In the case of Local Authority personal social services, it is not the department which is the employer, but the Local Authority, and departmental control over some of these aspects of personnel policy and practice may be very limited. Nevertheless, some latitude exists even there, and some of the ideas and practices developed in industry and commerce may be useful. This can be illustrated from the fields of employment, of training and of welfare.

First, the employment function is taken to incorporate the development and implementation of policies for the recruitment and deployment of the work force, including promotions. Underlying this is the idea that whereas people are recruited individually, the totality of the membership of an organisation constitutes an organisational resource which should be constructed and deployed to the best advántage overall. In its functions in relation to employment, personnel management is clearly there to service the organisation.

More technically, matters such as job descriptions and employment interviewing are part of an expertise which is available for non-specialists to draw upon. In a discussion of job descriptions Rosemary Stewart[26] for example suggests that many managers find it easier to think about personalities than about jobs, and that whatever the uses of a job description to a newcomer, the preparation of it forces the compilers to ask what they want a newcomer to do, what sort of a person is required to do it, and how the new job will fit in with existing ones. On the matter of employment interviewing Cuming,[27] for example, presents a framework for a recruitment procedure which, although it clearly cannot be applied to social work services as it stands, both illustrates how systematically such a procedure can be constructed, and embodies ideas which are certainly transferable to such services.

Second, there is the idea that staff once recruited represent a potential which should be developed, and that responsibility for education and training is an administrative rather than essentially professional function. Starting with the responsibility for finding and placing training officers, this function, according to Cuming, includes the induction and job training of all new entrants and, perhaps most significantly, the development of potential supervisors and managers. This conception of the training function appears to be a much broader one than that which is traditional in social work. Training is perceived as a matter of organisational significance, and consequently as an administrative responsibility. It is to be aimed not at particular occupational groups, but at any from whose more effective performance the organisation could benefit.

Third, the idea of responsibility for welfare, with which personnel management began, still finds a place in it. Welfare may be interpreted as a matter of a good physical environment and w rking conditions, or the provision of amenities, or help and support in the case of individual problems; or of concern that employment should, in so far as is possible, provide opportunity for individuals to develop their own aspirations and further their own ambitions. The general point to be emphasised is that whatever more philanthropic motives may accompany the promotion of welfare, this is organisationally a matter of making employment more congenial, and of encouraging people to stay. 'Welfare' is properly an administrative function, whether for specialists or not. At every level of an administrative hierarchy, it can be argued, responsibility for the work of others should be accompanied by a recognition of, and a responsiveness to, their needs.

To sum up, personnel management is an organisational, or administrative function to do with recruiting and deploying and keeping people. The nature of the organisations in which social workers are employed may preclude the employment of personnel specialists: and indeed specialists may not be needed. But this is not to say that the personnel function itself is irrelevant. Rather it may need to be considered as intrinsic to any organisation, in whatever ways the responsibilities for implementing it are to be allocated.

Public relations

As this discussion of administration has so far implied, there can be no objective definition of administration, and no one acceptable form for it to take. Prescriptions for administration are, however, probably most logically to be derived, as it is hoped that this discussion has illustrated, from concepts of organisation. For example, the ideas of organisations as closed bureaucracies and of administration as a means of control complement each other. Here, however, organisations have been presented as open systems, interacting with external environments which make demands upon them, which sanction their continued existence, and from which the resources which they need have to be recruited. If this is indeed part of the reality of organisations, then it is to be reckoned with as a pervasive factor in the situation with which administrators have to work. It means that administration is not simply an internal affair. Not only do administrators have to keep one eye on the present and another on the future: they must also simultaneously have in mind both the internal and the external significance of any particular action.

'Public relations' is here taken to refer to what administrators must do in order to establish and develop understanding between the organisation and its public. As in the case of personnel management, in some organisations a specific public relations function may be assigned to specialists. In others, it can be incorporated into the general administrative process, and then becomes the proper responsibility of all those who hold positions from which organisation and public are or should be in contact. Even the existence of specialists, however, does not mean that the function can be self-contained: for it can be said that whenever a member of an organisation is in contact with a member of the public on that organisation's business, he is its representative. The positions at which contacts of this kind occur will depend upon both the nature of an organisation's work, and upon the way in which it is internally structured. Before these two points can be explored, however, it is necessary to pose two questions about the nature of an organisation's public.

First, who constitutes this public? To this question, the response must be that an organisation is likely to have not one public, but many; as the situation of a Local Authority Social Services Department may serve to illustrate. Its publics include taxpayers, ratepayers, clients, potential clients, pressure groups, citizens who define the delinquent or the subnormal in residential care as unacceptable neighbours, or indeed any vocal or dominant section of a relevant population. Public relations thus becomes a balancing act in which conflicting attitudes and values have to be both acknowledged and handled. Similar problems face the Supplementary Benefits Commission: 'the letters which arrive by the hundred each month complaining that we hand out too much in social security benefits and support too many layabouts and scroungers, rarely come on headed notepaper from the leafy suburbs. Most of them are written by ordinary voters and taxpayers'.[28]

Second, one must ask whether, and if so how, an organisation's publics are to be directly involved in its decision-making processes. As far as Social Services Departments are concerned, the question highlights the implications of the essentially political context within which such departments operate, and of their positions within the super-system of local government. An objective made explicit in the Seebohm[29] report was to increase citizen participation in the planning, organisation and provision of social services, including 'the working out of democratic ideas at the local level' and 'the identification of need, the exposure of defects in the services, and the mobilisation of new resources'. Even so, writing in 1975 of community workers employed in Local Authority Social Services Departments, and having noted their particular sense of commitment, Harry Specht[30] comments as follows: 'I have not found one of them who has considered the question of how he might structure the participation of clients or potential clients into the decision-making systems of the social services departments'. A factor contributing to this situation may be that the problem of making progress towards the Seebohm Committee's objective is both political and organisational, as well as professional in the social work sense of the term. Its resolution implies the identification of publics other than local electorates, as well as modifications not only of client/worker relationships, but of the traditional triangular arrangement of citizen, elected representative, and local government officer.

The responsibility for handling such complex situations falls, it has just been suggested, at points which are a function of an organisation's work and of its structure. Illustrations can be drawn from industry, from the administration of Supplementary Benefits, and from Local Authority Social Services Departments.

In a factory, the operators who actually turn out the goods, and who are also at the bottom of the formal hierarchy, are doing work in which both contact with the organisation's public, and the need for such contact are minimal. Public relations are a matter for specialists in this particular field, or for sales managers and others at the upper end of the management structure.

In the administration of Supplementary Benefits, those who are also at the bottom of a formal hierarchy are doing work which involves constant contact with one particular public, variously described as clients, applicants or claimants, in a climate of opinion to which 'ordinary voters and taxpayers' contribute. Behind them, both literally and metaphorically, is a bureaucracy the majority of whose members are sheltered from such immediate contacts. As has already been indicated, however, clients are not the Supplementary Benefits Commission's only public. A public relations function with additional publics in mind is a matter of national policy as well as of day-to-day administration. Thus the chairman of the Commission announced,[31] in an open letter, that henceforth it will be more active in explaining its policies and informing the public about needs in its field. It would be interesting to monitor the implementation of this policy of greater openness, and to explore its implications for administrators at regional and local levels.

Like the Supplementary Benefits scheme, the personal social services of Local Authorities are publicly sponsored and publicly financed, and in each case the public relations function has a political dimension. As in the administration of Supplementary Benefits, those who literally administer the personal social services to members of the public are at the bottom of a line structure; but in this case they embody the organisation's main professional expertise. They are a two-way link between clients and organisation, representing the one to the other. Other publics, and other functions in relation to these publics, assume importance for other positions in the 'middle' or at the 'top'. But such is the open nature of a Social Services Department that to describe an Area Officer, for example, as being in the 'middle' of the organisational structure is to ignore a major characteristic of a position which may require that as much work be done outside the formal organisation as within it.

In some types of organisation, the major objectives of 'public relations' will be to create a market for the organisation's products. In others, the tasks will be much more to explain and publicise the nature and purposes of the organisation's work; to forestall criticisms of the organisation, or if necessary to respond to them; to enhance its 'image'; and to encourage public support for it, or use of it. These are essentially ongoing and local tasks to be undertaken within individual organisations, and which the public relations activities of professional associations such as BASW may supplement but cannot replace.

Monitoring and evaluation

Administration is to do with servicing and provisioning organisations so that they can function more effectively in the present, and with steering them into the future: it is concerned both with their maintenance and with their development. It represents an attempt to ensure that behaviour is as rational as can be, in the sense of being consciously directed towards objectives which have, in so far as this is possible, been consciously selected. But rationality in administrative behaviour does not stop with attempts to clarify objectives, or with decisions to deploy resources in certain ways rather than others. It also calls for the monitoring of the ways in which work is being done and plans are being implemented, and for attempts to evaluate results.

Such monitoring and evaluative functions logically include the supervision and evaluation of the work of individuals, and these are processes which are, to varying degrees, familiar to social workers as elements in their professional development. Here it is their organisational significance which must be emphasised. The individual who is being supervised or whose work is being evaluated is not an independent contractor, but someone in whose activities the roles of professional and of employee have to be combined. The supervisor occupies a position in which he is, in the words of Dorothy Pettes,[32] 'an "organisation man" in the best sense of the term . . . whose primary function is administration'. The nature of his work must be determined by the needs and the demands of the organisation as a whole, into which the 'professional' element is incorporated.

The supervision of workers by seniors may be perceived as being of concern primarily to the individuals whose professional development it may promote. Without denying the importance of this aspect of it, one can see it also as an administrative process through which supervisors monitor and evaluate work which is being done on the organisation's behalf, and ensure as fully as they can that resources in the form of professional skills and time are being deployed as effectively as possible.

When once monitoring and evaluation are seen as organisational processes, it becomes clear that it is not only to individual performances that they are to be applied, and not only at supervisory levels that administrators are involved in them. They apply to policies and to programmes at whatever administrative level responsibility for particular policies and programmes lies.

Ray Johns[33] suggests that systematic evaluation or appraisal has certain distinct uses. It clarifies the extent to which objectives are being achieved, providing a base from which improvement can be planned and programmes be modified as needs are perceived to have changed; stimulates the interest of those who participate in the evaluation process; contributes to the store of knowledge upon which work can be based; constitutes a response to a sense of social responsibility and accountability; and provides a basis upon which an organisation can justify its existence and its activities.

Given that these reasons for developing systems of evaluation are sound, the administrator is still left with the problem, which may be particularly difficult in service organisations, of identifying precisely what it is that is to be evaluated, the criteria by which success or failure is to be measured, and the forms which appraisal processes are to take.

Evaluation must be taken to include the evaluation of objectives; always supposing that objectives can be identified and isolated. This is a matter for judgment of value (ought we to be pursuing this purpose rather than that?) which cannot be quantified, but in the formulation of which rational concensus or agreement to differ can be sought. It is a matter also for judgment of efficiency (are particular short-term objectives the most effective means to long-term ends?). But how is effectiveness itself to be evaluated? Its measurement requires that subjective opinions be replaced by standards of both quantity and quality, each of which, but the latter in particular, may be difficult to specify.

Evaluation as an aspect of administration seems to require the simultaneous employment of two complementary approaches. The first is a technical one, to do with the development of objective criteria by which both the quantity and the quality of output can be measured. The second is the development of what Johns[34] describes as a questioning, analysing, judging and critical attitude of mind, which prompts the administrator continuously to question whether objectives are adequately defined, whether work is being done well, what are the nature and causes of particular shortcomings, and how performance might be improved. Particularly in service organisations, this attitude of mind must surely incorporate a continuous concern both to review and to evaluate the purposes which the organisation's work is serving. The impossibility of universal agreement about the objectives of social policy absolves neither the administrator nor the social worker from responsibility for attempting to assess the effectiveness of the work he himself is doing, according to his own values.

Conclusion

It is impossible to arrive at any universally valid description of the content of administration, and this chapter is prefaced by the assertion that there is no one best administrative method. In practice, administration involves taking decisions about what needs to be done, and how best to do it, in the particular situations in which individuals find themselves. Nevertheless, if action is to make sense, it has to be based upon a conscious assessment both of the situation in which action is to be taken and of the purposes action is intended to serve: and this requires the use of a frame of reference external to the unique situation immediately in question.

This particular discussion of the nature of administration has been intended to provide one such frame of reference. A level of generality has been aimed at which is sufficiently broad to indicate the existence of elements common to administration whatever the type of organisation in which it is practised. At the same time, the intention has been to illustrate that different types of organisation, and indeed differing perceptions of the same organisation, are significant for the forms which administration either does or should take.

The content of the main body of the chapter is also intended to constitute support for the idea that administration is a specialist activity, and that both theoretical knowledge and skills which are different from those which may be the source of expertise in holders of 'production' or 'staff' positions are relevant to it. This particular quality of administration may be unappreciated, or unrealised, for a variety of reasons. Administration may be associated in people's minds with routine clerical or bureaucratic activities. It is widely the case that people holding administrative positions have had no special training; and they may themselves think of administration as a limited and uninspiring kind of activity. In many organisations, promotion to an administrative position may be an award for creditable performance in a productive capacity, and be desired for no other reason; or it may provide round holes into which square pegs from other round holes are placed. It is implied here, however, not only that administration is a specialised activity, but also that it is potentially a worthwhile and positive one. This further implies that whenever professionals, whether they be doctors, social workers, engineers or teachers move into administrative positions, they are assuming roles which demand the application of knowledge and skills which are different from those with which their primary professional education and experience have equipped them. However useful this particular education and experience may continue to be, as administrators they are doing a different job, and have different perspectives on situations and different factors to take into account in making their decisions.

The question of whether administrators should be qualified in the profession which is basic to an organisation's work seems to be a matter of endless debate. The law required that Medical Officers of Health should be doctors. The Seebohm Committee[35] considered that 'no single profession in local government at present combines the ideal range of skills which will be required of the head of the [Social Services] departments', but that the aim should be to recruit people qualified in social work, with administrative experience and, if possible, training. As an addition to the debate, it can be suggested that the most rational approach to a conclusion about appropriate qualifications, is to start from a consideration of the nature of the work to be done. At supervisory level, it could reasonably be said, competence in the professional activity which is being supervised is essential. At organisation-directing level, the special competence which is required is very different: what is needed is not a good doctor or social worker or engineer or teacher, but a good administrator.

This assertion, however, calls for one particular comment on what constitutes a good administrator in a service organisation, whatever the position he holds. This comment has to do with his attitude towards the professional activities upon which the work of the organisation depends. First, the good administrator must be willing to acknowledge the special expertise of professional members of the organisation, and actively seek to involve them in planning and decision-making processes. As a corollary of this, he must know, and be continuously willing to learn, as much about current professional practices and concerns as his administrative support for professional activities requires. Second, and perhaps more importantly, his personal commitment must be not to the organisation as an end in itself, but to the services which it is the work of professionals to implement.

The existence of such a commitment will not mean that all conflict between administrators and professionals can be avoided or resolved. As was discussed in chapter 1, and is implied in much of what has been said about social services, about organisations, and about administration, employment in organisations inevitably modifies the behaviour of professional people. It makes particular demands and imposes particular restraints. But it also provides sanctions and resources, and if the idea of service to professional activities is incorporated into administrative practice, and is seen to permeate it, any validity which the equation of administration with bureaucracy may sometimes have is diminished.

However, if good administration involves a positive response to professional concerns, corresponding responsibilities fall on those who occupy roles which may be described as professional. There is a need for them both to attempt to understand the worlds within which administrators work, and to acknowledge the administrative significance of their own positions.

At the level of greatest generality, perhaps the main points to be emphasised are that administration is about the creation of policies, the development and maintenance of machinery for translating them into practice, and the review and evaluation of performance; that it is a conscious, deliberate and rational process; that correlations are to be sought between theories of organisation and prescriptions for administration; and that administration is properly a matter of concern to all those who have interests in the purposes which organisations can be developed to serve. Lest this discussion of the nature of administration may have made it all sound tidier than real life can ever be, or than one would perhaps wish it to be, it may be as well to counterbalance it with the idea that although greater rationality may be a desirable objective, it is also an elusive one: 'what is laid down, ordered, factual, is never enough to embrace the whole truth' and 'life always brims over the rim of every vessel'.[36]

Chapter five

Social work in organisations

In the administration of social services, compulsion must be made
compatible with consent; mass production with variety; conformity
with adaptability; and above all, efficiency with human sympathy.

T. S. Simey

So far throughout this book, direct references to social work as an
aspect of organisational activity have been intentionally rationed. The
discussions of professionalisation, of social services and of public
administration, of organisations and of administration as an organisational process, have been intended to emphasise two main ideas. The
first of these is that if social workers restrict themselves to a
professional frame of reference, they are adopting too narrow a base
from which to attempt to understand the nature of social work as it is,
as distinct from what they may think it ought to be. The second is that
whatever its own particular attributes, social work is not an altogether
unique activity. Their employment in organisations means that social
workers share with other occupational groups problems and opportunities which are organisational rather than professional in origin. The
emphasis has been on the general rather than the specific, and on the
nature of professions, of organisations and of administration, rather
than directly on its significance for social work in particular. It now
remains to shift the focus onto social work, and to explore the
implications for it of the organisational contexts within which social
workers have to attempt to give expression to their ideas of how it
ought to be done.

To begin with, one further reference must be made to the nature and
the implications of distinctions between the 'is' and the 'ought'. It is
implicit in the ideas presented in chapter 1 that social work in Britain is
unlikely ever to become a fully-fledged profession in the traditional
sense, and in chapters 2 and 3 that the nature of social work is
politically, publicly, socially and organisationally as well as profession-

ally determined. The other side of the picture is that social workers are themselves continuously evolving their own ideas about what social work ought to be like. These two perspectives, however, constitute only different sides of the same picture, and they are not so much alien to each other as in continuous tension.

What social work ought to be like is not a matter for consideration here: it is properly a matter for debate by social workers themselves and, one might add, by parliament and public. Whatever social workers think they ought to be doing, however, and whatever methods they think they ought to be using, in the majority of cases both their tasks and their methods have to be implemented and developed from within the social services, and the organisations, in which they are employed. A discussion of the implications of this will constitute the subject matter of this chapter. The method will be to use ideas presented in chapters 1 to 4 to examine the kinds of situations in which social workers, employed as they are in large and complex organisations which are components of public social services, may have to work. Local Authority Social Services Departments will be taken as proto-types; but it is hoped that the issues discussed will be of sufficient general relevance as to mean that those whose particular concern is with organisations of a different kind, will be able to make extrapolations for themselves.

It is assumed that a social worker's motivation, in whatever type of organisation, will derive from an identification with social work as he thinks it ought to be, and that his primary concern will be the provision of the best service possible to his clients. It may be logical to begin with a consideration of the position from which the social worker in a Local Authority Social Services Department has to attempt to translate this concern into practice, and of the significance of this for his role as a social worker.

It is as likely as not that if such a social worker were asked to describe his position, he would define it as being on the bottom rung of an hierarchy within a bureaucracy. These two terms indeed seem to dominate discussions by Local Authority social workers of the organisational situations in which they find themselves: and not without reason. For example, the relationship between social worker and Director is essentially a line relationship, and moreover one in which a number of positions in a vertically arranged formal structure are interposed between the social worker and the Chief Officer. Social workers may rarely if ever see the Director. The discretion allowed to them is limited and, beyond its limits, it is through the line that they have to seek authority and resources for doing what they wish to do. The line is a system through which orders and instructions come down to them, through which they are made aware of the force of rules and regulations, and through which they may be held accountable for behaviour which they might wish to regard as of professional rather than administrative concern. They may be harrassed by forms to be filled in, by decision-taking processes which are formal and cumbersome and in which the urgency of the needs of individual clients appears not to be recognised, and so on. Above all, they may feel themselves oppressed by a dead-weight of bureaucratic attitudes and methods of work, whether amongst 'office' staff or amongst holders of positions in the middle of the ladder, or at the top, whom they believe to have lost sight of social work values and objectives.

All Social Services Departments are clearly permeated by phenomena such as these and, as far as one can see, inevitably so. For social workers to say that they are employed in hierarchical and bureaucratic systems is thus to reflect the truth: but only part of it.

One may stop to consider whether this perception by social workers of the organisations in which they work reflects the most significant characteristics of these organisations; or whether it is prevalent because ways of looking at large and complex organisations other than as bureaucracies or hierarchies do not so readily come to mind.

If one were to examine different sections of any one Department, one would almost certainly find that some were more bureaucratic than others; and if one were to compare one Department with another overall, the outcome might well be similar. If having examined the form taken by a particular Department or part of it this year, one were to examine it at some point in the future, one might find it to be more, or possibly less, bureaucratic than it was. Such possibilities imply that to refer to an organisation as a bureaucracy is to describe it very imprecisely indeed; and as the content of chapter 3 was intended to indicate, it is safe to say that no large organisation is a bureaucracy and nothing else. The implication of this is that a social worker's organisational position is not simply at the bottom of a bureaucratic ladder, and that in order to understand it one must attempt to identify what kind of an organisational animal a Social Services Department is.

In the light of the ideas presented in chapters 1 to 4, the plan for the rest of this chapter is to consider first Social Services Departments as organisations; second, the significance for professional aspects of their work of the positions in which Local Authority social workers are employed; and third, administration as a means of curbing the unwanted qualities of organisations, and of developing those that are believed to be constructive.

Social Services Departments as organisations

It would seem to make sense to acknowledge first of all that Social Services Departments display all the attributes of 'ideal type' bureaucracies. Having made this assertion, one must go on to qualify it, beginning with a reiteration of the points just made. Some sub-sections of any one Department may be less bureaucratic than others; some functions within a Department may be less bureaucratically organised than others; not all the characteristics of the 'ideal type' will be equally developed; and the bureaucratic features of any one Department will change over time. It is thus not important to ask whether or not a Social Services Department is or is not a bureaucracy. Rather must one explore in each case the forms which bureaucracy takes; the purposes which particular bureaucratic features serve, and those for which they are dysfunctional; and the possibilities of controlling their development accordingly. Each of these points may be illustrated in turn.

First, bureaucracy may not take the same form in all Departments, in the sense that its various characteristics may not all be developed to the same degree. In all Departments there are hierarchies or lines of authority from Director to producer, whether the producer be a social worker, or a houseparent, or a clerk. Where social workers or houseparents are concerned, the line also constitutes an accountability system from those who are in direct contact with clients to the Director, who is accountable to his employers. It is probably a tenable argument that the nature of the legislative responsibilities vested in Social Services Departments means that this particular feature of bureaucracy is unavoidable. But even in Departments of similar size, the number of rungs in such hierarchies may vary and so, most significantly, may the extent to which decision-making authority is delegated downwards throughout them. Although hierarchies may exist universally, they are not uniform in the ways in which they are used as systems of control; and in any case 'hierarchy' is not synonymous with 'bureaucracy'. Other phenomena such as a clear-cut definition and allocation of duties, an emphasis on rules and regulations as a source of authority, and formality and impersonality in administration are also contributions, but in each case in varying degrees, to the bureaucratic nature of any large organisation.

Second, each aspect of bureaucratic organisation may be useful for certain purposes and harmful to others, or efficient in certain circumstances but not in others. To say this is to suggest that the bureaucratic features of Social Services Departments are not to be judged good or bad either in their entirety, or as though there was only one purpose to be served. An hierarchy of authority and accountability may mean that decisions are taken more slowly than social workers would like, but it may also serve to check idiosyncracies, and to further the equitable allocation of available money, or of residential places, amongst the whole of the relevant clientele. It also constitutes a structure through which responsibility is shared. Written rules may be seen as a restriction of the professional autonomy of social workers, but they also afford protection and are sanctions for ensuring that certain work is done which might otherwise not be done.

As organisations are essentially instruments for the co-ordination of the work of many individuals, some restriction of individual autonomy is unavoidable; but a rationalisation of work may in some cases increase efficiency and in some cases decrease it. One problem is that bureaucratic efficiency is of a different order from professional efficiency, and bureaucratic methods may be used effectively for some aspects of a Department's work, but not for others. Additionally, some members of a Department will tend to find bureaucratic methods congenial whereas others will not. Once again, the problems lie not so much in the nature of bureaucracy as such, but in the extent to which appropriate restraints can be placed upon its development, and in the impact which bureaucratic methods may have on particular purposes. A filing system, for example, is in essence a bureaucratic device, but it may be designed so as to serve either bureaucratic or professional purposes; or possibly even both. In general, the 'growth of bureaucracy' may constitute a major social and political problem of our times. In the case of Social Services Departments, generalisations are inappropriate. The practical problems are specific ones, to do with the sources of bureaucratic controls, and with the possibilities both of checking bureaucratic methods before they become ends in themselves and of using them, and sometimes even developing them, to serve more acceptable purposes.

There is a sense in which existing conditions are defined as problems only if there is some possibility of ameliorating them, and what has just been said implies that at least some of the negative aspects of bureaucracy can, to some extent, be controlled. Third, therefore, is the idea that 'bureaucracies' are not static, but are both subject to and amenable to change. As the concept of professionalisation is both broader and more dynamic than that of a profession, so bureaucratisation as distinct from bureaucracy embodies the idea that even in their more formal aspects, organisations are processes in which change is endemic. Each of these terms might be taken to imply that development is in one particular direction. Harry Specht,[1] however, has discussed the idea of the deprofessionalisation of social work; and it is useful to bear in mind that a particular organisation, or parts of it, may go through processes of debureaucratisation. For example, the authority to make certain decisions may be decentralised; or an organisational structure may be devised which allows greater diversities to develop within particular sub-systems such as Divisions or Area Offices; or record-keeping systems may be modified so that they are more effective for professional purposes; or supervision may be made less close; or those in managerial positions may develop enabling rather than controlling attitudes. If therefore Local Authority social workers are employed in organisations which are bureaucratic, they are also holding positions of which even the bureaucratic aspects are not fixed but both heterogeneous and dynamic, and in some respects at least amenable to modification.

Not only does the idea of a bureaucracy as it applies to a Social Services Department demand qualification, but any realistic concept of such an organisation must also embody the notion of change, or of process. Change may be planned or unplanned; it may develop from within or be imposed from outside; it may result from initiatives taken with the future in mind, or it may be determined by events already in the past. If social workers feel the heavy hand of bureaucracy, an equally significant force may be that of ceaseless change. Like a profession, a Social Services Department needs to be recognised as a process with no foreseeable end. It is also a process of which the precipitators are not only individual people but also events, and which may manifest itself in changes not only in individuals but in procedures, methods, and structures. There is no possibility that a Social Services Department can ever arrive at an equilibrium either internally or in relation to its environment, or in terms of people or of structures or procedures.

One of the products of bureaucratic methods of organisation may be a set of prescriptions for action which persist irrespective of the comings or going of individuals, as in a routine established for decisions relating to Place of Safety Orders; or for payments under C and YP (1969) Section I; or for the allocation of places in Part III accommodation; or for claiming travelling expenses or overtime. Thus, and in many less formal ways, stability is built into a Department's life. But between stability and change there is perpetual tension, which administration represents an attempt to manage, but which it can never completely relieve. The phenomenon of process, embodying change, development, evolution, progress, transformation, innovation, growth or decay seems no less characteristic of Social Services Departments than do bureaucratic modes of organisation.

Burns and Stalker[2] have considered it relevant to distinguish between organisations under conditions of comparative stability and of environmental change, and have suggested that such differences are significant for the ways in which they should be managed. If social workers tend to ignore the dynamic or 'process' element in Social Services Departments while emphasising the 'bureaucratic' one, they may be reinforcing the idea that management is by definition bureaucratic.

To the notion that Social Service Departments are bureaucracies has now been added the idea that they are processes. Furthermore, like any other organisation, they must be considered as systems. Two main points surface immediately, and may be looked at in turn. First, they are open systems, and second, they are systems which are composed of an intricate complexity of sub-systems.

The first observation to be made is that the existence of a title should not be taken to imply the existence of a self-contained or autonomous unit of organisation. A Social Services Department has no identity which is independent of the super-systems of which it is a part, or of the environment in which it is contained and which impinges upon it. Even if it is perceived essentially as an hierarchical structure, the hierarchy does not end within the Department, but extends into the administrative and political super-systems of local government, upon which the Director is dependent for resources and to which he is accountable. But a concentration on the hierarchical structure as presented for example in an organisation chart, produces a one-dimensional picture in which a whole network of relationships with the environment are grossly under-represented. A Social Services Department might be more appropriately pictured as floating in an environment which both controls and sustains it, upon which its existence depends, and only through innumerable contacts with which can its work be done.

The 'openness' of a Social Services Department is both a matter of fact and a problematic issue, in so far as both the degrees of openness and the forms which it takes are of both professional and political significance. An important corollary of it is that the forces which social workers may feel as restraints are as much political in nature as bureaucratic. They are significant in terms of work, resources, sanctions, controls and objectives.

To begin with, external factors are significant determinants of much of the work which a Department has to do. First, for example, a Local Authority and therefore a Social Services Department may legally do nothing which an Act of Parliament does not either require or permit it to do, and changes in legislation, and the forms which it takes, constitute one of the most significant determinants of the ways in which Local Authority social workers spend their time. Second, the workplace itself is to a considerable extent outside the physical location of the Department, in what social workers (like missionaries?) tend to call 'the field', and with people in the roles of clients who are not themselves members of the organisation, but who influence, and participate in defining, the form which work takes. Local Authority social workers are employed in organisations of which the work is extensively determined by legislation and by statutory instruments, by the edicts of departments of central government, by Local Authorities and their committees, and by particular categories of members of the public including the clients who bring work to them. To say this is not to deny their own part in defining work, but only to emphasise the significance for the ways in which they do so of the open, and in some important respects the subordinate, nature of the organisational systems in which they are employed.

Second, a Social Services Department is an open and dependent system in the matter of resources. There is no market in personal social services, and no return on a Department's product which it can invest in its own development. It is in this respect also part of the super-system of local government, the responsibilities of which are very much broader than the provision of personal social services. If not part of a market system, it is nevertheless part of a competitive one, in which resources are scarce in relation to the demands made upon them. It is directly dependent for resources upon its particular super-system of local government, and it is open to the impact of the restraints under which the super-system is itself working. In manifold and less direct ways, it is also open to the influence of current social and political attitudes towards the super-system of social services representing the 'welfare state'.

Third, a Social Services Department is an open system as far as sanctions go. The specific sanctions under which social workers work may originate from within the Department itself; or they may be found in legislation or in the policies of a Local Authority or its committees; or in public attitudes and values, either local or more widespread, which sanction the activities of social workers, at least in the sense of tolerating or ignoring them, until points are reached at which tolerance is withdrawn, and the force of 'public opinion' has to be acknowledged. In such an open system, the activities of members of an organisation have to be considered not only in professional terms, or in terms of their significance organisationally, but on the basis of the response which they produce externally.

Fourth, the external origins of work, of resources and of sanctions imply the existence of external controls. It is not only a fact but also an intention of public policy in relation to local government, that those who are employed in public services should be subject to some degree of control. It is of the nature of a Social Services Department that it is an agency not only in the social work sense of the term, but also of the Local Authority. Some of the controls under which its members work are bureaucratic in so far as they originate from within the administrative as distinct from the political sector of local government, or because they are intended to serve bureaucratic ends. But the origins of others, even if they take bureaucratic forms, are essentially political and are, therefore, to be differently evaluated and differently managed. It can be argued that what goes on within departments of local government is less open to public scrutiny and control than is democratically desirable, and that too much control over major decisions has passed from elected representatives to those whom they employ. An implication for social workers as distinct from those who make top-level policy decisions, may be that social work is to be seen not exclusively as a form of professional activity to be defended against external criticisms and controls, but as a process in which these have to be acknowledged as legitimate elements in the implementation of public social services.

Fifth, there is the problematic matter of organisational goals and objectives. The more closed a system is, the more these can be determined internally. In an open system they are matters of controversy and of variations in interpretation over a wider front and, to varying degrees, a function of external influences upon the ways in which resources are made available or work is defined, or of the operation of external sanctions or controls. Universities are examples of organisations which are becoming more open, in a variety of ways. For example, the extent to which they should or should not be producing graduates to serve industry is a matter of public debate, and it is probably true that they are less free than they were to determine their purposes for themselves irrespective of the significance of national policies in higher education. Social workers might possibly agree that the purposes of a Social Services Department should be to meet individual need as they and their clients think best; but the sorts of need to which they can in practice respond, the formal categories into which clients are placed, and the kinds of control which social workers may be expected to exercise, are legally, publicly, politically and socially as well as professionally determined.

This presentation of Social Services Departments as systems has been intended to emphasise their dependence upon particular super-systems, and also their openness; and in conclusion the point may be stressed once again that they are essentially political institutions, and part of a publicly sponsored social service. If bureaucratisation is a problematic issue, so also is the balance at every point between departmental and specifically professional autonomy, and public intervention.

If a Social Services Department is an open system dependent upon other systems, it is all too clearly not an internally homogeneous one. Especially in a book intended for social workers, it is all too easy to concentrate attention on teams of social workers and hierarchies connecting their positions to that of the Director, with the consequential risk of relegating other sub-systems to the background. As in the case of relationships between the Department and the outside world, however, the idea of a network rather than of an hierarchy may be important; and particularly the idea of a network of interlocking sub-systems rather than of individuals. The first, and most obvious, point to be made is that a Social Services Department is an extremely complex network of sub-systems; and this is a factor which may be much more significant organisationally than its size in terms of the number of people employed.

It may be possible to identify particular sub-systems based on the nature of the work to be done, or on the skills involved, or on a geographical area, or on a particular building; but like the larger system which is the Department, they have no autonomous identity. An individual Community Home is part of the Department's system of residential provision for children, which in turn is part of its child care function, which is implemented through the sub-system into which social work is organised; to say nothing of its links with a regional system. The interdependence of such sub-systems serves to illustrate once again the inadequacy of the concept of hierarchy to describe the kinds of relationships through which work in a Social Services Department has to be accomplished. The position of Team Leader may be used as an hypothetical example. A Team Leader heads a sub-system in the form of a team, and holds a position in an hierarchical system from social workers to Director; he may be expected to acknowledge the staff authority of a Training Officer or of a Chief Administrative Officer in certain non-operational matters; and the social work function of his team cannot be implemented without access to services such as residential care, which are organised in yet another different sub-system from his team.

Different sub-systems within any Department may have different kinds of work to do, compete with each other for resources, use different technologies and methods of work, operate on differing ideas of what constitutes efficiency, be based on different kinds of authority systems and be subject to different kinds of control, incorporate significantly different norms and values, and to varying degrees constitute distinct sub-cultures within the Department as a whole. Some of these sub-systems may be categorised as operational in so far as responsibility for the actual production of services is vested in them; whereas others such as training or research sections or student units, or sub-systems responsible for office organisation or for finance, are not themselves implementing services to clients, but have to interact with those sub-systems which are.

The complexity of the work to be done within a Social Services Department demands the creation, maintenance and modification of sub-systems throughout which this work is allocated. Relationships between people in different sub-systems are complicated enough, although they can perhaps be clarified if holders of different positions are understood as needing to relate to each other on a number of different bases which can be formally defined, but which are not necessarily hierarchical. But equally complicated are relationships between the sub-systems themselves, which are constituted not only of people but of work.

Social Services Departments have been discussed as bureaucratic organisations, as processes, as identifiable but dependent and internally heterogeneous open systems, as elements in a public social service, and as having dimensions which are significantly political. This has not been an exhaustive application to them of all the ideas about organisations presented in chapter 3, but what has been said so far may at least provide a basis for a consideration of the significance of employment in a Social Services Department for the position which social workers have to hold. Some still outstanding ideas about organisations, such as the co-existence of formal and informal elements, their technologies, and organisational typologies, will enter into this, and into the analysis of administration which is still to come.

Position of the social worker

An idea which has been intended to permeate the whole of this book is that however social workers wish to implement their roles, in a Local Authority setting these roles are shaped by the positions which social workers hold as employees within complex formal organisations which are part both of a public social service and of the system of local government.

It is perhaps worth reflecting that the two forms of social work which were most highly professionalised before 1970 were medical social work and psychiatric social work. The practitioners of these two specialisations, as far as their statuses as employees went, and with the exceptions of a small number of psychiatric social workers, were able to identify themselves as members of interdisciplinary working units, in hospitals or child guidance clinics, rather than as employees in organisations which impinged upon them as bureaucracies. Nor, again with a small number of exceptions in Local Authority Health or Welfare Departments, were they implementing formal statutory functions.

The trend towards the employment of social workers to implement the statutory functions of Local Authorities began with the creation of Welfare Departments and Children's Departments in 1948, and might be regarded as one of the most humane developments of the welfare state. But the culmination of this trend in the Local Authority Social Services Act (1970) may have had political consequences for social work of a very fundamental kind, for the Act set the seal on a situation in which for as far ahead as one can see, and with the exception of the Probation Service, a virtual monopoly in the public employment of social workers was created for Social Services Committees and Departments. Social legislation creates social work services, and sanctions the activities of social workers and the provision of resources; but it is at the same time a significant factor in determining the overall structures of the organisations within which social work roles are implemented, and in defining the content of those roles.

138

Thus the first point to stress about the positions of social workers in Social Services Departments is that these positions are in organisations which are publicly sponsored, financed, controlled and administered. Much of the day-to-day work of social workers is unheralded and unsung, if only because it is uncontroversial from a public or political point of view; but it has been suggested (p. 52) that the discretion upon which social workers draw does not belong to them as of right but has been delegated to them. Their positions are exposed to public criticism and possibly to public action if the discretion is considered to have been misused. These then are positions in which professional and public elements co-exist, and are intended to do so.

A by-product of this is that the social worker's position is in a structure of authority and accountability. The hierarchy from social worker to Director may be felt to be a bureaucratic device through which controls are exercised over professional activity. Rowbottom[3] describes it otherwise. He refers to the tendency of social workers to assume that 'agency' values are in conflict with 'professional' ones and that the latter are always better, but suggests that a Social Services Department is to be seen as 'an executive arm of democratic government' and, moreover, that if it was not wished that professionals should work professionally, they would not be employed. Rowbottom thus sees the hierarchy not specifically as a system of control, but as one through which authority and discretion are delegated and, most importantly, accountability is concentrated. The existence of a hierarchy in itself tells us nothing of the way in which a particular Department is managed: its 'managerial style' may be formal and authoritarian, or informal and democratic. What a hierarchy does do, according to Rowbottom, is to locate the social worker's position in relation to an apex at which accountability for all that goes on beneath comes home to roost. The social worker's position is to this extent a protected one, in so far as actions which are potentially critical are based on decisions which are not taken by the social worker alone, but are made or sanctioned by his organisational superiors. Unlike the Probation Officer, the social worker in a Social Services Department is not individually and directly accountable to his employers for his work with particular clients: the social worker's formal position is one in which his immediate accountability is to his team leader, in an hierarchical system in which a perennial administrative problem is the maintenance of appropriate balances between control as an instrument of accountability, and the delegation of authority as an instrument of an individual social worker's autonomy in a professional capacity.

If the position is one in which it is intended that a social worker can be called to account for his work, however, it is also one in which in so far as he views himself as a professional person, he will consider himself individually and personally responsible for the standard of social work service which he offers to clients. Some of the tensions within the position have thus to do with balances not just between accountability and autonomy, but between the social worker's statuses as employee on the one hand, and as an individual wishing to assume personal and professional responsibilities on the other.

If the work to be done by Social Services Departments were neatly divisible into clear-cut specifications; if all social workers within each specialisation were equally knowledgeable, skilled and experienced; or if all Departments were equally bureaucratised, the task of defining the position of Local Authority social workers in a system of accountability and responsibility would be both theoretically and practically simpler than it is. As such uniformity does not exist, no comprehensive definition is possible. The position is part of an hierarchical structure, but the forms which the structure may take in individual organisations are highly variable.

Moreover, the hierarchical structure of accountability of which the social worker's position is typically perceived as the bottom rung cannot itself be adequately described in bureaucratic terms, and one of the variables is the extent to which such systems are in practice permeated by professional attitudes and values. For example, the accountability and authority structure in which the social worker holds a position is also a communication system: information and instructions and guidance come down, but information, ideas and pressures can also be channelled upwards. It is furthermore a decision-making system; and the extent to which social workers perceive their positions as incorporating elements of these two aspects of organisational life, in addition to an element of control, may be significant for the ways in which they attempt to use these positions.

If the social worker's position is at the bottom of a line structure, it is also the position from which much essential work of the organisation is performed. Herein lies a dilemma. In a factory, it is typically the least skilled productive work which is done at the bottom end of the line. In a Social Services Department, the reverse is the case. This is not to say that those who hold top management positions, or staff positions such as those occupied by training officers, are not highly skilled in their own particular spheres. But a professional base upon which the quality of output to individual clients depends is undeniably that of social work; managers and staff officers are by definition not producers; and those in whom a variety of skills which production requires are embodied are, if Social Services Departments are perceived in strictly bureaucratic terms, at the bottom of the ladder.

The openness of Social Services Departments as well as their internal structure is, however, it may once again be emphasised, a significant determinant of the nature of the social worker's position. This may be described as being a 'front-line' position in a number of ways. It is a position in which responsibility for the delivery of the services which the Department is there to provide is vested. It is a position from which work is done outside the formal organisation, both literally and in the sense that this work is both with and on behalf of people, in the roles of clients, who are not members of the organisation. It is a front-line position in the sense that its holders, whether individually or collectively, are exposed to criticism, from committees or the press or members of the public, to an extent from which positions which might be described as being further 'inside' a Department are protected. It is an exposed position from which, because they are employed to act as members of the organisation, social workers may not be freely able to defend their behaviour, but one in which they are dependent upon the organisation for support when they consider this to be needed. On the other hand, however, the positions held by social workers as main performers of the organisation's primary task, and from which they have a very major share indeed of direct contact, very often in private, with the organisation's clients, may also be described as front-line in Dorothy Smith's sense of the term (see p. 83). It has already been suggested (see p. 105) that an organisation's work can be said to consist of what is done as distinct from what is professed as being done: and to the extent that social workers constitute a major component of a Department's direct work force, they occupy positions from which the day-to-day implementation of their roles as producers to whom discretion is available, may be a factor which persistently modifies formally established policies and practices. On this point, it can also be said that as social workers constitute a significantly large occupational group within any Department, certain front-line characteristics of their positions may endow them, collectively if not as individuals, with a power which undue emphasis upon their low ranking in hierarchical terms may serve to disguise.

Thus, it is suggested, the public or political characteristics of Social Services Departments, their openness, and the nature of the work to be done, as well as any bureaucratic attributes which they may develop, all influence the nature of the positions from which social workers have to act. An additional characteristic is their nature as systems which are not internally homogeneous, but which consist of complexes of interacting sub-systems. This means that the position of a social worker needs to be defined not only in relation to a Team Leader and thus up through the line to Director, but in relation also to such positions as those of receptionists, typists, the staff of residential, day care and domiciliary services, and indeed of a whole range of specialist services upon the co-operative availability of which the provision of a satisfactory 'social work' service may depend. In organisational terms, it is a position from which relationships have to be maintained not only with peers and with 'line' superiors, but with service givers and other specialists.

Once again, nothing has been said about the prescriptions for practice which are incorporated into social work theory, or about what social workers think should be the purposes and the content of their relationships with clients. The point to be emphasised is that whatever these ideas may be, in the case of the majority of social workers they have to be translated into practice from positions within formal organisations.

Such organisations as Social Services Departments impose restraints and controls, and add an extra-professional factor to the very nature of social work. They are also sources of support and of resources, and the positions which social workers hold as members of them constitute points of leverage which, given that social workers are extensively dependent upon employment within a Local Authority setting, they need to be able to use actively and possibly aggressively within the organisation itself, if professional purposes are to be promoted.

Tension is unavoidable. The nature of their employment within statutory social services means that social workers may have to meet certain demands and accept certain restraints which would not otherwise impinge upon them. Employment within large and complex organisations likewise puts curbs on individual autonomy of a kind which the freelancer or the member of a compact face-to-face working unit does not have to accept as part of the reality of his working life. On the other hand, the Local Authority social worker is employed not only as an agent for the implementation of specific pieces of legislation, but presumably also in the expectation that his primary concern will be for the welfare of those members of the community of whose needs he is professionally conscious. Employment within statutory social services and within organisations is as much part of the reality of social work as is the social worker's competence in working with clients. It may be that in the long run, the skills of social workers in working within and in influencing and modifying very complex organisations, may be as crucial to the welfare of clients as are their more specifically professional abilities.

The problem is a daunting one. As long ago as 1937 T. S. Simey[4] very unequivocally expressed his concern about the negative impact upon the users of social services of the ways in which those services were administered: 'The existence of the mechanism necessary to carry out in practice a complete range of social services may even be found to be in many ways incompatible with the ideas of political liberty on which the political life of Great Britain is founded.'

Since the time when Simey was writing, it is probably safe to say, social policies have become very much more humane, and social work itself has developed into a significant element in their administration. Concurrently, the social services have expanded not only in scope and in intention but also in complexity, and problems to do with the administration of effective services to individuals through the agency of complex organisations may have changed, but seem unlikely to have diminished. An attitude in which the employing organisation is summed up as 'the bureaucracy' which impedes the social worker's implementation of his 'professional' role, is in this situation a denial both of the reality and of the potentialities of the organisational situation, and of the administrative responsibilities which are part of the package of employment within a statutory social service.

In chapter 4 a distinction was made between producers and administrators: between those whose work consists of the actual output of goods or services and those whose work is to do with the organisation of production. The distinction holds for Social Services Departments: social workers, home helps and so on, are producers, whereas those to whom they are accountable are administrators. Nevertheless, social workers may be said to carry administrative or organisational responsibilities of various kinds. For example, they may be responsible for defining or supervising the work of social work assistants or of volunteers or of typists. Within the limits of discretion available to them they administer the use of their 'own' time and skills. Moreover, as it is the whole intention of this book to argue, they *ought* to consider themselves not simply as producers upon whom the organisation impinges, but as active participators in organisational affairs, for sound professional reasons.

To say this is to adopt the view, also expressed in chapter 4, that administration is something different from clerical work, and that it is not simply a bureaucratic process but one which can be directed towards ends which are deemed to be more important than the organisation itself. If a creative type of administration is indeed possible, being an organisationally conscious social worker calls for an approach which is more positive than the reluctant acceptance of organisational restraints; and becoming an administrator need not involve a defection from a commitment to social work values and objectives. On the assumption that administration can be a positive process, the rest of this chapter will consist first of a discussion of the nature of administration as a specialised activity within a statutory social work service and second, of the participation of social workers in it.

Administration in Social Services Departments

(a) The administrator's role
The framework upon which this discussion of a potential role for administrators in Social Services Departments is based is to be found in

chapter 4, which in turn drew upon the discussion of the nature of organisations in chapter 3. First, the foundation for it is the idea that administration is a specialised activity, for which a theoretical basis is to be sought in such understanding as is possible of the nature and uses of organisation. Although administrators can be social workers at heart, their positions give them different perspectives on situations from those of social workers, and their work is different from that of social workers and calls for the use of different knowledge and different skills. Second are the ideas that although each organisation differs from every other there are characteristics which all organisations share, and that although styles of administration both can and should be adapted to specific situations, administration also incorporates elements which are universal. To this extent it is possible for administrators to make their own special sense of administration, as social workers as distinct from the lay public make their special sense of social work. The concept of administration which has been developed so far, is taken to incorporate the roles of Directors and Team Leaders alike; but as in any one organisation the specific tasks which the implementation of each of these roles requires so obviously differ, the focus will be on common elements which typify the 'administrative situation' within which the administrator, whether he be responsible for the functioning of the whole system or for only a part of it, has to clarify and develop his particular role from his particular position.

A classical prescription for administration in relation to social work is to be found in a curriculum study published by the American Council on Social Work Education[5] and may be summarised as follows. Administration is primarily a problem-solving process, involving the identification and analysis of problems, and the formulation, implementation and evaluation of plans for their solution. It is concerned primarily with 'futures', it calls for the use of value-judgments in the selection of alternatives, and it involves the creative rather than the routinised use of knowledge and skills. It is an enabling process, concerned with facilitating maximum efficiency through the creation of appropriate structures and through helping groups and individuals to work co-operatively and effectively. It is concerned with the creation of appropriate balances between standardisation on the one hand and the creative use of human resources on the other, and the administrator's stance is one in which particular problems are viewed in relation to their significance for the functioning of the organisation as a whole. Especially in public services it is concerned to a greater or lesser extent with implementing the public will, and 'a major aspect of professional judgment in administration in social welfare is that there is often either a conflict of public wills or the public will is not clearly formulated'.

With the possible exception of the last point this prescription is sufficiently generalised to be applicable to almost any organisation of any type. Something at least a little more specific to administration in Social Services Departments may be built onto it using some of the ideas which have been presented so far about the nature of public services and public administration, of organisations and of the nature of administration as an organisational process. To begin with, one may consider how a Social Services Department is to be typed.

First, it is a public organisation. Whatever their positions in the formal structure, administrators in Social Services Departments are administering a public service with all the implications of the points discussed in chapter 2. For example, public wills, public values and public attitudes are intrinsic to the administrator's frame of reference, and in much of his problem-solving and decision-making activities he must take them into account. Additionally, specific forms of control may be imposed from outside in the shape of formal rules and regulations which it is not within his discretion to reject, and the implementation of legislation may call for the creation and implementation of structures of accountability which are more formal than any his personal predilection would lead him to organise. Moreover, the very nature of the work which administrators may define as being either necessary or permissible, and the grounds upon which priorities are determined, are extensively a function of the legislative duties and powers which are the basis of the Department's existence and of the public origins of its resources.

Second, such an organisation may be typed as a particular sort of public organisation: as a department of local government, incorporating features which it inevitably shares with other such departments and which may impose upon its administrators ways of working which they would not otherwise choose.

Third, it may be classified as a service organisation in so far as its manifest function is to provide services to those members of the public for whose welfare public provision is intended to be available. This is both a realistic and a congenial way of typing an organisation of which social work is a major professional activity: but unless it is applied critically, it may serve to disguise some of the conflicts with which administrators may be confronted. For example, they are administering services in which the bases upon which people are defined as being eligible for service may be politically and publicly determined, either nationally or locally, and may not correspond to categories of need as either administrators or social workers perceive it. Additionally, in some aspects of the organisation's work, the service function co-exists with a commonweal function of protection for the public, as specifically in certain cases of mental illness or of juvenile delinquency, and more generally in the protection which the forms taken by legislation give to dominant social values. It may sometimes fall to the administrator to accept the significance of these commonweal functions, and to tilt the balance of decisions in ways which social workers might not wish to do.

Fourth, a Social Services Department may be typed on the basis of the roles and statuses of those of its members who identify themselves with a profession. If it is accepted that the functions of such a Department are social and political as well as professional, and if the reality of political, legislative and organisational controls over the activities of social workers is acknowledged, then a Social Services Department cannot be described as a professional organisation. It was suggested in chapter 1 that the 'ideal type' concept of a profession offers only a very incomplete guide to the professional identity of social work; and Etzioni's notions both of semi-professions and of semi-professional organisations may provide more realistic indications of the nature of Social Services Departments. As a corollary of this they may be typed in accordance with their basic technologies, including that of social work as practised by an occupational group with strong if controversial professional commitments and aspirations.

As has been emphasised throughout the book, there can be no objective definition of organisations, and attempts to describe them must not be taken for the reality. Other ways than those just suggested may be found for typing Social Services Departments in general. Additionally, individual departments may fit typologies which have less to do with their nature as sub-systems of statutory social services than with their own peculiar characteristics as ultimately unique organisations. For example, if a 'front-line' organisation is one in which the real power to influence policy lies with members at the periphery and at the bottom of a line structure, some departments will be found to conform to the type more closely than do others.

The four characteristics identified above are suggested as being generic to all Social Services Departments as sub-systems within statutory social services, and as of overriding significance for those who administer them. Each department also manifests in its distinctive ways those attributes of formal organisations which were discussed in general in chapter 3, and with specific reference to Social Services Departments on pp. 130–3. Administrators are thus working with social institutions which may be represented as incorporating aspects of 'ideal type' bureaucracy; as dynamic processes exposed to and amenable to change; as systems linked to super-systems and themselves internally heterogeneous; as interacting with an external environment; as incorporating goals and work to be done; as dependent upon resources and upon particular technologies; as incorporating particular norms and values; and in which both human and impersonal factors are determinants of behaviour.

Such attributes of organisations constitute the reality with which administrators must work. An acceptance of their significance means that administration can be attributed with dimensions which are appropriate to organisations of whatever kind. Such an idea was the foundation for the general discussion of administration in chapter 4 which in so far as it is relevant to any organisation, is relevant to a Social Services Department.

To make this assertion is by no means to deny that particular types of organisation such as Social Services Departments present particular administrative problems and require the application of particular administrative methods. Nor, however, has it been implied that administration is a stereotyped form of activity; and the idea that there is no one best way of administering an organisation deserves re-emphasis. This having been said, it is assumed that administration in Social Services Departments implies positive involvement in organisational life as discussed in chapter 4, with adjustments to the needs of particular departments as they are perceived by particular administrators at particular times.

This assumption in turn embodies three interlocking ideas: that administration involves the making of choices about both ends and means, that it is a conscious and active rather than a passive kind of process, and that the choices available to administrators, in Social Services Departments as elsewhere, include choices of administrative style.

No matter what position an administrator in a Social Services Department holds, some discretion is available to him to decide how to make use of it. His choices will in no case be unrestricted, but some scope will be available to him to decide what factors to take into account in making particular decisions, and what methods to employ. He may perceive administration as an essentially technical activity, or as an essentially normative one in which his choice of administrative methods and techniques is consequent upon his value judgments both about the objectives which he considers the organisation or his 'own' part of it ought to be serving, and about the ethical legitimacy of alternative ways in which those objectives might be pursued.

It has been suggested (p. 126) that effective administration in a service organisation involves the commitment of the administrator both to the service function and to the professional activities upon which the implementation of that function depends. This suggestion could be taken to refer simply to a technique of administrative practice. It is intended rather to imply a value judgment that the commitment should be a personal one. This alone carries the implication that administration in Social Services Departments not only is but also ought to be an essentially normative activity. The commitment of administrators to the purposes of social workers will not produce an end to tension and conflict, and a narrow commitment to social work is administratively unworkable. But something which is possibly remediable is wrong in situations in which social workers believe that administrators have 'forgotten what social work is about', and in which they in turn have little appreciation of the work which the maintenance and development of their particular organisation involves, and of the pressures which administrators face.

The demands and the potentialities of the social worker's role in relation to administration are yet to be discussed, but something remains to be said at this point about the relevance or otherwise of particular administrative styles to the nature of the work which Social Services Departments have to do and which it is the specialised task of administrators to further.

The ways in which administrators behave can be influenced by such factors as their ideas of what organisations are like, of what they can be like, of what they ought to be like, and of the possibilities of using administrative positions to influence what goes on inside them. An administrator may choose to view his position as one in which he himself is subject to controls from above, and emphasise his own accountability for what his subordinates do: he may perceive the organisation in essentially bureaucratic terms, and act accordingly. At the other end of the spectrum he may kick against the pricks of organisation for as long as he can, and try to identify himself exclusively with a particular occupational activity, such as social work. Yet again he may both consider a bureaucratic concept of organisation to be too narrow to be realistic, and ascribe to himself as an administrator, whatever his position in a line structure, a much more active and positive role than that of an agent through whom predetermined policies are implemented or hierarchical forms of control imposed.

An example of affinities between a particular concept of organisation and methods of administration is offered by Sayles[6] who presents what he considers to be the managerial implications of an open system model.

Sayles's first point is that a manager cannot pick and choose his own particular 'style' of management at will, but must take his clues from the requirements of the work to be done. Many styles may be needed, ranging from the exercise of tight controls to a very liberal delegation of authority. For example, certain situations may call for tighter controls than do others, and so may certain kinds of work; and certain individuals may prefer to work under clear and specific direction while others feel a need for freedom of a kind which the first group could not tolerate. The administrator has not to decide once and for all whether to adopt a strong line or a permissive one, but rather to be ready to judge what is appropriate to any particular situation.

Second, a systems approach to administration calls for acceptance of the idea that the objectives embodied within an organisation are multiple and often incompatible, and continuously changing. The administrator cannot assume the possibility of unilinear activity directed towards a goal which all members of the organisation and of its super-systems share, but must live and work with imprecision, and with disagreements about what should be done and how. Sayles sees him not as making key decisions of heroic proportions, but as dealing continuously with uncertainty and with ambiguity, as involved in action which is reciprocal rather than one-sided, as monitoring what goes on rather than expecting that final points will ever be reached.

Third, Sayles suggests that a systems model incorporates the ideas of shifting boundaries between both groups and activities. This in turn implies mutual dependencies and a willingness to accept the absence of compartmentalised and static responsibilities. The administrator must see the handling of change as an integral part of his job and, moreover, be willing to accept the initiation of change from 'below' and to seek to convince higher management if change is needed.

This example of affinities between ways of looking at organisations and ways of administering them is anything but bureaucratic, and it has indeed been selected to illustrate that administration is not *per se* a bureaucratic activity. Social Services Departments manifest in varying degrees most of the attributes of ideal-type bureaucracy, some of which may be useful and some not. But they are not simply bureaucracies, and to become an administrator in one of them is not necessarily to become a bureaucrat, but to assume a position from which choices can be made within a reality which is both more complex and more open to modification than any which the concept of bureaucracy can possibly encompass.

The administrator's work in a Social Services Department is different from that of the social worker, whether the administrator in question be a Team Leader or the Director. The administrator is not himself doing social work in the sense of being the mediator of services to clients. His perspective on situations and the information which he possesses are different from those available to social workers, and the factors which he both can and should take into account in making his decisions are different. He works with 'the organisation' or with part of it, and the skills and techniques which he needs to make use of are thus different from those of the social worker. Although the need for a commitment to the purposes of social work has been stressed, the administrator is directly confronted with the organisational as well as the professional implications of translating this commitment into practice. To describe administration in a Social Services Department as a method of social work[7] is thus to interpret its nature too narrowly, and to ignore the existence of tensions which are inescapable. Nevertheless, social work is impossible without the organisations which it is the work of administrators to structure and to sustain, and

Social work in organisations

administration can be, and be seen to be, a means whereby the greater effectiveness of what social workers are trying to do is ensured.

Once administration in a Social Services Department has been defined as a specialised activity, however, it becomes necessary to emphasise that it is not a matter for administrators alone. Unless they are content to try to encase themselves in a cocoon of relationships with individual clients or with 'communities' while grumbling about the oppressiveness of 'the administration' or of 'the hierarchy', social workers must be prepared to accept responsibility for learning how organisations work and about the restraints and the opportunities which membership of an organisation carries with it. They cannot escape the impact on their work of the organisation in which they are employed and it would seem to make sense that rather than leaving administration to 'them', or hoping that it will go away, they should attempt to participate actively in influencing the form which organisation takes and the effects which it has. Thus in conclusion, this discussion of the nature of administration in Social Services Departments shifts from the role of the administrator to that of the social worker.

(b) The administrative role of the social worker

Social workers in a Social Services Department are no more and no less employees in organisations than are administrators, although their positions and their roles are different. Although their professionalism influences their responses to organisational matters, it does not exonerate them from responsibility for co-operative participation in a collective enterprise. Conformity with particular policies and practices is demanded of them; their positions locate them within an accountability structure; and the forms which professionalism might otherwise take are modified by the requirement that they should implement their roles as employees.

While not an administrator in the specialist sense, the social worker inevitably participates in administration in a number of ways. He holds a position in the administrative structure of the department. What he is able or required to do is influenced by the form which that structure takes and by the ways in which it works. He does his social work as a representative of the organisation and not only as a professional person. He uses discretion which is organisationally delegated to him. He administers to clients services which are sanctioned by the organisation; and he directly manages the ways in which he makes use of the time and skills which are at his disposal. Additionally and most importantly, he may add another dimension to this conservative interpretation of his administrative role, and comprehend the organisation not only as something to be responded to or resisted, or left to administrators to

150

manage, but as an instrument which social workers can use. Thus, if administration impinges upon the social worker, it is also a process in which he participates and which he can attempt to influence. And if political, public and organisational factors are significant determinants of what professional social work both is and ought to be like, providing that the existence of such realities is acknowledged there is scope within employing organisations for social workers to bring their own particular concerns to bear. It is for such reasons that an understanding of the equivocal concept of a profession and of the nature of statutory social services, of organisations and of administration seems as relevant to the role of a social worker as is training in methods of working with clients. Indeed training in such methods themselves would seem to call for a consideration of their implications in organisational terms: for surely while the implementation of even the more traditional forms of case-work is problematical within an organisation which is part of the structure of local government, more politically radical methods of social work, and more radical attitudes on the part of social workers produce distinctive problems and call for particular skills in the use of the organisational context in which Local Authority social workers have to function.

References to administrative aspects of the social worker's role and to the organisational dimensions of particular methods of social work bring us directly to the question of education in administration for social workers as distinct from administrators. In an article in which he argues for the better-informed participation of social workers in ensuring the effectiveness of the whole organisation, Anthony Hall[8] points to a distinction between training for the assumption of particular managerial or organisational roles, including the learning of appropriate techniques, and education of a broader kind 'concerned with questioning many of the basic assumptions currently held about how organisations do and should function, how work gets done, and how decisions are, or might be made'. Hall regrets that the report of the working party on manpower and training for the social services[9] makes but a brief reference to training for management; and as far as the training of social workers is concerned, the assumption seems once again to be that the content of education and training can be adequately defined in 'professional' terms. The argument which it has been the intention of this book to promote is that social workers *as social workers* need to know as much as they can about what organisations and the administration of them are like and can be like, and to develop their own ideas of what they ought to be like and of how they can be used and improved. This applies irrespective of the particular service in which social workers are employed. Attention here has been centred on Social Services Departments, but in their own particular ways Probation Officers and social workers in voluntary organisations, whether long-established ones or those which are still in the first stages of growth, also face organisational problems and opportunities for creating or modifying organisations to meet intended purposes. If the specifics are different, the basic questions to be posed and the basic factors to be taken into consideration have their origin in such characteristics as all organisations may be said to share.

One characteristic of organisations is that they are in varying ways and to varying degrees permeable, and social workers may use their front-line positions to exert a direct influence upon what goes on in them. There is also a factor with a longer-term significance. It tends to be from the ranks of social workers that administrators are recruited and it may be useful that, as social workers, administrators of the future should have begun the task which Anthony Hall[10] identifies of overcoming prejudice and resistance to management theory, and of breaking free of perceptions of it which are rooted in outdated notions of 'scientific management' and of bureaucracy.

Within organisations social workers are restrained, but they are also enabled. Without such organisations as those which are the creations or the by-products of social policy most of them would be powerless, for they would have no resources and no positions from which to act. These organisations are not just to be responded to, but to be used.

The quotation at the head of this chapter dates from 1937[11] and its original reference was specifically to the administration of social services to their users. Its appropriateness in this respect has not diminished, but at this point in time it seems to constitute a prescription which is as relevant to the internal administration of any organisation of which social workers are members as it is to contacts between members of those organisations and clients. If it originally posed problems which are now more than ever implicit in the task of providing individualised services through the agency of large organisations, it may also perhaps be construed as implying a responsibility for the quality of social service organisations which should not be left to administrators alone, but in the assumption of which social workers themselves should attempt to play an informed and active part.

Suggestions for further reading

As was declared in the introduction, one intention of the book is to point to the existence of a range of potentially relevant material which has no common source and which has not been incorporated into the acknowledged literature of social work itself. References to such material have thus been made very freely throughout the text and are listed on pages 155–61. Collectively they illustrate how wide is the field to be draw upon, and how knowledge which may be directly relevant to an understanding of the organisations in which social workers are employed has already been systematically developed over many years in a number of disciplines such as sociology, public administration and social administration.

The following suggestions for background reading are also to be taken with this in mind.

On professionalisation

Elliott, P., *The Sociology of the Professions*, Macmillan, 1973.
Etzioni, A. (ed.), *The Semi-Professions and their Organization*, Free Press, 1969.
Papers by Greenwood, A., and by Bucher, R. and Strauss, A., in Zald, M. (ed.), *Social Welfare Institutions*, Wiley, 1965.
Jackson, J. A. (ed.), *Professions and Professionalisation*, Cambridge University Press, 1970.

On public administration and on the political context of social work

Brown, R. G. S., *The Management of Welfare*, Fontana, 1975, which is particularly useful for locating the statutory social services, including the personal social services, within their governmental context and for illustrating the interconnectedness of the processes of 'social' and 'public' administration.

Hill, M. J., *The Sociology of Public Administration*, Weidenfeld & Nicolson, 1972.

Lees, R., *Politics and Social Work*, Routledge & Kegan Paul, 1972.

On organisations

Etzioni, A., *Modern Organizations*, Prentice-Hall, 1964, is a compact and readable introduction to the development of organisation theory and to problems and methods of management.

Perrow, C., *Organisational Analysis*, Tavistock, 1970, is lively and undogmatic and is 'intended for those who need to know something about organisational behaviour in order to manage, or survive in, organisations'. Its cheerful scepticism is incorporated into a lucid discussion of the general concepts of organisational structure, technology, environment and goals which it should be possible for social workers to relate to their own organisational situations.

On administration as an organisational activity

No one complete text on methods of administration seems appropriate for isolated mention. However, L. R. Sayles, *Managerial Behaviour*, McGraw-Hill, 1964, chapter 14, is useful on two counts. It illustrates very succinctly affinities between ideas of what organisations are like and appropriate methods of administering them; and it presents a prescription for administration which is a denial of the idea that it is an essentially bureaucratic activity.

A study of social service administration in practice which illustrates both its significance for the implementation of intended policies, and the unreality of the idea that professional activities can be self-contained, is to be found in A. S. Hall, *The Point of Entry*, Allen & Unwin, 1975.

References

Preface

1 N. Glazer 'The limits of social policy' in P. Weinberger (ed.), *Perspectives on Social Welfare* (2nd ed.), Macmillan, New York, 1974, p. 254.
2 C. Churchman, *Systems Approach*. Delta, New York, 1968, p. 29.
3 D. Silverman, *The Theory of Organisations*, Heinemann, 1970, pp. 26 et seq.
4 A. Greenwood, 'The attributes of a profession' in M. Zald (ed.), *Social Welfare Institutions*, Wiley, New York, pp. 509-23.

Chapter 1   The concept of professionalisation

1 H. Witmer, *Social Work: An Analysis of a Social Institution* Rinehart, 1942, P. 11.
2 A. Greenwood, 'The attributes of a profession' in M. Zald (ed.), *Social Welfare Institutions*, Wiley, New York, 1965, pp. 509-23.
3 P. Halmos, 'The personal service society' in *British Journal of Sociology*, vol. 18, no. 1, March 1967.
4 H. Witmer, op. cit., p. 6.
5 N. Toren, 'Semi-professionalism and social work' in A. Etzioni (ed.), *The Semi-Professions and their Organization*, Free Press, New York, 1969, p. 106.
6 See, for example, A. M. Carr Saunders and P. A. Wilson, *The Professions*, Oxford University Press, 1933, pp. 284-7.
7 A. Greenwood, op. cit., p. 522.
8 M. L. Cogan, 'The problem of defining a profession' in *Annals of American Academy of Political and Social Science*, 1955.
9 P. Elliott, *The Sociology of the Professions*, Macmillan, 1973. (See introduction in particular for a sociological approach as distinct from the social work orientation of Greenwood.)
10 Ibid.
11 R. Bitensky, 'The influence of political power in determining the

theoretical development of social work' in *Journal of Social Policy*, vol. 2, part 2, 1973.

12 R. Bucher and A. Strauss, 'Professions as process' in M. Zald (ed.), *Social Welfare Institutions*, Wiley, New York, 1965, pp. 539-53.

13 Ibid., p. 540.

14 Ibid., pp. 549-50.

15 A. V. Dicey, *Law and Opinion in England in the Nineteenth Century*, Macmillan, 1948, p. lxxvii.

16 M. C. Arden, 'National Health Insurance' in *Social Welfare Forum*, Columbia, 1973, p. 134.

17 A. Greenwood, op. cit., p. 522.

18 A. Etzioni (ed.), op. cit., Preface.

19 N. Toren, in ibid., pp. 147-50.

20 A. Etzioni, *Modern Organizations*, Prentice-Hall, 1964, p. v.

21 See *Social Work Today*, vol. 4, nos 17, 18, 21, 1973, for motion on registration of social workers passed at Annual General Meeting of BASW, 1973, and subsequent correspondence.

22 See P. Leonard, 'Social workers and bureaucracy' in *New Society*, vol. 7, no. 192, 2 June 1966.

23 See O. Stevenson, 'Knowledge for social work' in *British Journal of Social Work*, vol. 1, no. 2, 1971.

24 See discussions at BASW conference, *Social Work Today*, vol. 4, no. 17, 1973.

25 See discussion paper, 'Eligibility for membership', *Social Work Today*, vol. 6, no. 9, 24 July 1975.

Chapter 2   Social services and public administration

1 K. Boulding, 'The boundaries of social policy' in W. E. Birrell (ed.), *Social Administration*, Penguin Books, 1973 and T. H. Marshall, 'Voluntary action' in *Sociology at the Cross Roads*, Heinemann, 1963, chapter XVI.

2 See R. Lees, *Politics and Social Work*, Routledge & Kegan Paul, 1972.

3 R. Titmuss, *Essays on the Welfare State*, Allen & Unwin, 1958, p. 39.

4 I. Berlin, *Two Concepts of Liberty*, Oxford University Press, 1958, p. 54.

5 R. Titmuss, *Commitment to Welfare*, Allen & Unwin, 1968, p. 23.

6 See J. Handler, *The Coercive Social Worker*, Markham, Chicago, 1973.

7 R. Holman, 'The place of fostering in social work' in *British Journal of Social Work*, vol. 5, no. 1, 1975.

8 Children Act (1948), Part II, 12.

9 G. Green, 'Politics, local government and the community' in *Local Government Studies*, June 1974, pp. 5-16.

10 S. Finer, *Anonymous Empire*, Pall Mall, 2nd ed. 1966, p. 3.

11 Idem.

12 Ibid., p. 112.
13 *People and Planning: Report of the Committee on Public Participation in Planning,* HMSO, 1969.
14 *Report on Local Authority and Allied Personal Social Services,* HMSO, Cmnd 3703, 1968.
15 G. Green, op. cit.
16 *Report on Local Authority and Allied Personal Social Services,* para. 491.
17 For analyses of the nature of public administration, see for example: R. G. S. Brown, *The Administrative Process in Britain,* Methuen, 1971, and R. J. S. Baker, *Administrative Theory and Public Administration,* Hutchinson 1972.
18 P. Self, 'Elected representatives and management in local government, an alternative view' in *Public Administration,* Autumn 1971.
19 *Report of the Committee on the Management of Local Government,* HMSO, 1967, vol. I, paras 1 and 2.
20 J. S. Mill, *Representative Government,* Dent & Sons, Everyman ed., 1960, p. 177.
21 M. J. Hill, *The Sociology of Public Administration,* Weidenfeld & Nicolson, 1972, p. 197.
22 *Report of the Committee on the Management of Local Government,* vol. I, para. 109.
23 P. Self, op. cit., p. 271.
24 Ibid., p. 277.
25 R. W. Rowbottom, 'Organising social services: hierarchy or . . .?' in *Public Administration,* Autumn 1973.
26 M. J. Hill, op. cit., p. 205.
27 O. H. Hartley, 'The relationship between Central and Local Authorities' in *Public Administration,* Winter 1976.
28 *Report of the Committee on the Management of Local Government,* vol. I, para. 224.
29 See, for example, R. James, 'Is there a case for Local Authority policy planning? ' in *Public Administration,* Summer 1973, and P. Self, 'Is comprehensive planning possible and rational?' in *Policy and Politics,* vol. 2, no. 3, March 1974.
30 *The New Local Authorities: management and structure,* HMSO 1973, para. 4.33.
31 A. Roberts, 'Boundaries of professional authority' in *Social Work Today,* vol. 5, no. 8, 1974.
32 H. Eckstein, *The English Health Service,* Oxford University Press, 1959, p. 157.
33 A. Roberts, op. cit.
34 Brunel Institute of Organisation and Social Studies, *Social Services Departments,* Heinemann, 1974, pp. 100-1.
35 For example, see BASW activity in relation to the Children Bill as described in *Social Work Today,* vol. 5, no. 25, 20 March 1975, vol. 6, no. 1, 3 April 1975.
36 Sub-Committee of the First Division Association, Professional Standards in Public Practice, in *Public Administration,* Summer 1972.

References

37 W. Beveridge, *Voluntary Action*, Allen & Unwin, 1948, p. 305.
38 E. Heath, 'The government and voluntary service' in *Social Service Quarterly*, Winter 1972.
39 *Hansard*, House of Lords, col. 1170, 9 February 1972.
40 *Report of the Charity Commissioners for England and Wales*, quoted in *Journal of Social Policy*, April 1972, p. 177.
41 G. Murray, *Voluntary Organisations and Social Welfare*, Oliver & Boyd, 1969, p. 17.
42 Ibid.
43 E. Heath, op. cit.
44 Children and Young Persons Act (1969) Section 39.
45 T. H. Marshall, *Sociology at the Cross Roads*, Heinemann, 1963, p.341.
46 W. Beveridge, op. cit., p. 304.

Chapter 3 Organisations

1 A. Pincus and A. Minahan, 'Towards a model for teaching a basic first year course' in L. Ripple (ed.), *Innovations in Teaching Social Work Practice*, Council on Social Work Education, New York, 1970.
2 For an exposition of scientific management and human relations approaches, see A. Etzioni *Modern Organizations*, Prentice-Hall, 1964.
3 O. Stevenson, 'Knowledge for social work' in *British Journal of Social Work*, vol. I, no. 1, 1971.
4 See B. J. Heraud, *Sociology and Social Work*, Pergamon, 1970. Part I and CCETSW Report, *Sociology in Education for Social Work*.
5 See, for example, P. M. Blau and W. R. Scott, *Formal Organisations*, Routledge & Kegan Paul, 1963, pp. 27-36.
6 D. Silverman, *The Theory of Organisations*, Heinemann, 1970, p. 11.
7 Ibid., p. 74.
8 See, for example, H. Stein, 'Administrative implications of bureaucratic theory' in *Social Work*, vol. 3, no. 4, 1961.
9 P. M. Blau, *The Dynamics of Bureaucracy*, Chicago University Press, 1955, pp. 201-14.
10 For example, W. Bennis, *Changing Organisations*, McGraw-Hill, 1966.
11 D. Katz and R. L. Kahn, *The Social Psychology of Organisation*, Wiley, New York, 1966, p. 61.
12 See P. Selznick, 'Foundations of the theory of organizations', reprinted in A. Etzioni (ed.), A Sociological Reader on Complex Organizations, Holt, Rinehart & Winston, 1964, pp. 18-32.
13 P. M. Blau and W. R. Scott, op. cit., p. 6.
14 P. Selznick in A. Etzioni (ed.), op. cit, pp. 19-20.
15 See for example, C. Argyris *Interpersonal Competence and*

Organisational Effectiveness, Tavistock, 1960 and D. McGregor, *The Human Side of Enterprise,* McGraw-Hill, 1960.
16 C. Perrow, *Organisational Analysis,* Tavistock, 1970, chapter 3.
17 D. Silverman, op. cit., pp. 73 et seq.
18 D. McGregor, *Leadership and Motivation,* Cambridge, Mass., 1966, quoted in D. Silverman, op. cit., p. 83.
19 A. Etzioni, *Modern Organizations,* Prentice Hall, 1964, p. 2.
20 Idem.
21 C. Perrow, op. cit., chapter 1.
22 Ibid., p. vii.
23 E. J. Miller and A. K. Rice, *Systems of Organisation: the control of task and sentient boundaries,* Tavistock, 1967, pp. xi-xiii.
24 See A. K. Rice, *The Enterprise and its Environment,* Tavistock, 1963.
25 A. Etzioni, *Modern Organizations,* p. 3.
26 C. Perrow, op. cit., p. 134.
27 Social Work (Scotland) Act, 1968, Part 11, 12.
28 See A. Gouldner, *Patterns of Industrial Bureaucracy,* The Free Press, New York, 1954.
29 P. M. Blau and W. R. Scott, op. cit., chapter 2.
30 C. Perrow, op. cit., pp. 27 et seq.
31 P. M. Blau and W. R. Scott, op. cit., pp. 45-57.
32 See A. Etzioni, *A Comparative Analysis of Complex Organisations,* Free Press, New York, 1961.
33 A. Etzioni, *The Semi-Professions and their Organization,* Free Press, New York, 1969, Preface.
34 T. Burns and G. M. Stalker, *The Management of Innovation,* Tavistock, 1961.
35 I. Goffman, *Asylums,* Doubleday, 1961.
36 D. Smith, 'Front-line organisation of a state mental hospital' in *Administrative Quarterly,* vol. 10, 1965/6, pp. 381-99.
37 P. M. Blau and W. R. Scott, op. cit., p. 43.
38 D. Smith, op. cit., p. 399. Effectiveness, Tavistock, 1960 and D.
39 A. Gouldner, op. cit., pp. 27-9.
40 A. Etzioni, *A Comparative Analysis of Complex Organisations,* p. 313.
41 C. Perrow, op. cit., p. 181.
42 A. Etzioni, *A Comparative Analysis of Complex Organizations,* p. 313.
43 D. Silverman, op. cit., p. 121.
44 Quoted in K. Mannheim, *Ideology and Utopia,* Routledge & Kegan Paul, 1954, p. 25.
45 P. Cohen, *Modern Social Theory,* Heinemann, 1968, pp. 170-1.

References

Chapter 4   Administration

1 R. G. S. Brown, *The Management of Welfare*, Fontana, 1975, p. 15.
2 In E. Reed (ed.), *Social Welfare Administration*, Columbia, 1961, pp. 14 et seq.
3 Joan Woodward, *Management and Technology*, HMSO, 1958.
4 H. A. Simon, *Administrative Behaviour*, Macmillan, New York, 1961, p. xv.
5 Idem.
6 See Brunel Institute of Organisation and Social Studies, *Social Services Departments*, Heinemann, 1974.
7 M. Kogan, *et al.*, *Working Relationships within the British Hospital Service*, Bookstall Publications, 1971.
8 M. W. Susser and W. Watson, *Sociology in Medicine*, Oxford University Press, 1962, pp. 156-62.
9 W. Brown, *Exploration in Management*, Penguin Books, 1960, p. 44.
10 T. Burns and G. M. Stalker, *The Management of Innovation*, Tavistock, 1961, chapter 6.
11 W. Brown, op. cit., p. 45.
12 Ibid., p. 44.
13 HMSO, *Management of Local Government*, 1967, para. 51.
14 See D. Stewart, *Management in Local Government*, Charles Knight, 1971, chapter 5.
15 E. Powell, *Medicine and Politics*, Pitman, 1966, chapter 4.
16 R. Parker, 'Social Administration and Scarcity' in E. Butterworth and R. Holman (eds.), *Social Welfare in Modern Britain*, Fontana, 1975, pp. 204-12.
17 See C. Barnard, *The Functions of the Executive*, Harvard, 1948.
18 T. Burns and G. M. Stalker, op. cit., p. 252.
19 See, for example, D. Katz and R. L. Kahn, *The Social Psychology of Organisations*, Wiley, New York, 1966, chapter 9.
20 H. Montgomery, 'The practice of administration' in *Child Welfare*, vol. XI, no. 2, 1962.
21 R. Parker, *Planning for Deprived Children*, National Children's Home, 1971, p. 13.
22 P. H. Levin, 'On decisions and decision making' in *Public Administration*, Spring 1972.
23 H. A. Simon, op. cit., chapter IV.
24 Ibid., pp. 45 et seq.
25 M. W. Cuming, *The Theory and Practice of Personnel Management*, Heinemann, 1968, p. 7.
26 R. Stewart, *The Reality of Organisations*, Macmillan, 1970, chapter 2.
27 M. W. Cuming, op. cit., chapter 4.
28 D. V. Donnison, in *Social Work Today*, vol. 6, no. 20, 8 January 1976.

29 *Report on Local Authority and Allied Personal Social Services,* HMSO, 1968, para. 491.
30 H. Specht, 'Community work in the United Kingdom' in *Policy and Politics,* vol. 4, no. 1, p. 000
31 D. V. Donnison, op. cit.
32 D. Pettes, *Supervision in Social Work,* Allen & Unwin, 1967, see chapters 1, 2 and 11.
33 R. Johns, *Executive Responsibility,* Association Press, New York, 1966, p. 108.
34 Ibid., p. 42.
35 *Report on Local Authority and Allied Personal Social Services,* para. 620.
36 B. Pasternak, quoted in I. Origo, *Images and Shadows,* Murray, 1970, p. 5.

Chapter 5   Social work in organisations

1 H. Specht, 'The deprofessionalisation of social work' in Paul E. Weinberger (ed.), *Perspectives on Social Welfare,* Macmillan, New York, 1974.
2 T. Burns and G. M. Stalker, *The Management of Innovation,* Tavistock, 1961.
3 R. W. Rowbottom, 'Organising social services; hierarchy or . . .?' in *Public Administration,* Autumn 1973.
4 T. S. Simey, *Principles of Social Administration,* Oxford University Press, 1937, p. 18.
5 S. Spencer, *Administration Method in Social Work Education,* Council on Social Work Education, New York, 1959.
6 L. R. Sayles, *Managerial Behaviour,* McGraw-Hill, 1964, chapter 14.
7 See for example S. Spencer, op. cit.
8 A. Hall, 'Bringing management down to size' in *Community Care,* 4 August 1976.
9 Department of Health and Social Security, *Manpower and Training for the Social Services,* HMSO, 1976.
10 A. Hall, op. cit.
11 T. S. Simey, op. cit., p. 10.